Yoni Mantras

An empress's guide to peace
within the heart, temple,
and sacred womb

Yoni Mantras

An empress's guide to peace
within the heart, temple,
and sacred womb

Jewel the Muse

Jewel Muse Publishing
Atlanta, GA

YONI MANTRAS
AN EMPRESS'S GUIDE TO PEACE WITHIN THE
HEART, TEMPLE, AND SACRED WOMB

This publication is designed to educate and provide general information regarding the subject matter, based on the author's experiences. The information included in this publication is not meant to diagnose, treat, or cure any disease. It is published with the understanding that neither the author nor the publisher is engaged in rendering professional or medical advice or services. Each situation is different, and the advice should be tailored to particular circumstances.

Paperback ISBN: 978-0-578-70014-4

Published by Jewel Muse Publishing
Atlanta, GA

Printed in the United States of America
First Edition July 2020

Cover Design: Travis Robeson
Interior Design: Make Your Mark Publishing Solutions
Editing: Make Your Mark Publishing Solutions
Cover Art: Julie Iris Design

Contents

Acknowledgements

I wish to express my gratitude to my beloved father, who has supported all of my dreams, loves me, and cares for me so deeply. I am beyond blessed to have your support in all of my endeavors and your everlasting and unconditional love.

I wish to express my deepest appreciation for my Mema. Since I was a child, you encouraged me to take excellent care of my heart, mind, body, and spirit. You taught me so much, and I promise to keep all of your lessons and wisdom close to my heart.

Anyone I've missed knows that I also love them deeply ...

Dedication

This book is dedicated to my honorable ancestors, and the Most High, Allah. I am forever grateful for this beautiful gift of life. Thank you for empowering me to walk in my truth and be my own expression of divinity.

I promise to make you proud and continue
this legacy in our name.

—Ciara

A poem for you….

"Goddess, Evolve"

Goddess, I've been expecting you.
I've held space just for you,
and I'm so blessed that you are finally here.

Goddess, you are admired—
all of your curves, dimples, and perfect imperfections,
your brilliance, luminosity, and radiance you never knew you had.

You are a walking masterpiece,
a muse.
You are sand, sunshine, and ocean waves,
paradise.

You're sweet.
You're soft.
You're blossoming like my favorite flower,
a rose; that's you.

Now I ask you,
rise with me on this journey deep within.
Heal with me.
Let's evolve together.

Goddess, evolve…

"Your womb is a sacred gift. At the base of your sacral chakra, it is the center of creation. You are the temple. Remember your divinity."

—Jewel

Introduction

Welcome, Empress. My name is Ciara, but I go by Jewel. I am a holistic and spiritual black queen who loves to write, vlog, relax, travel, and spend time in nature. I call myself a "Yogi and Pole Goddess" because I love practicing yoga and all forms of exotic dance. I am a huge advocate for feminine healing and manifestation, which is why I created Yoni Muse LLC. My brand is dedicated to helping women achieve peace within the heart, mind, body, and womb space. In 2018, I stepped into my passion and purpose of enlightening the goddesses who walk this universe. That's you. So, it is such a pleasure to meet you, and I am ecstatic about our upcoming evolution.

I thrive off of feminine energy, and I absolutely adore women. It is currently 12:23 a.m. I am snuggled up in my bed, relaxed and laid-back. Does this sound familiar? Are you in this same position? You might be, but you also might be out and about; you may have just busted this book open, or you may be doing none of the above.

Regardless, you made the decision to purchase *Yoni Mantras*, and for that, I am forever grateful. I want to acknowledge appreciation for every wombman who opens this book. Women mean so much to me, and I have dedicated my life's purpose to serving them, to serving *you*. Your support means so much, and it is a pleasure to embark on this enlightening journey with you. Regardless of if you know me personally or not, I am grateful you are here. I'll fly this plane if you agree to be my copilot. Thank you, Goddess. Thank you, Queen. Thank you, Empress.

The idea of *Yoni Mantras* came to me randomly one day. I felt a calling to enlighten and connect with women on a deeper level. This book will be the first of many to come, and with each addition, you are guaranteed to learn something you did not know before. I am blessed to have divine wisdom, knowledge and experiences to share with others. I recognize the need for more women empowerment, and the rise of divine feminine beings in this world. So here I am, writing this peace as if it were my own diary, hoping to inspire someone or educate another queen about her sacred pum pum.

Spirituality and Religion

I want to address something early in this book because I know spirituality is expressed in different ways. You may be non-religious, spiritual, or you may hold strong religious values, and that is perfectly fine. Regardless of your beliefs and faith, know that you were intelligently designed by the Most High, and your womb is a very special and sacred gift.

My goal isn't to tell anyone how to live their life or what to believe in. My goal isn't to show anyone the light or the path to success. My goal is to be the light and inspire others to illuminate themselves and create their own path. I want to share what has worked for me, changed me, helped me heal my wounds, and assisted me in becoming healthier and happier than I've ever been.

This realm is based on opinions, perspectives, and hidden truths. During your journey you will realize that the majority of our religious and spiritual teachings reflect the ultimate goal of love, truth and unity. Your spirituality is simply finding what path resonates with your heart and soul. You know in your heart what is true.

The term "New Age Spirituality" makes me laugh because spirituality is as ancient as can be. Spiritual practice helps us uncover the beautiful, joyful, and radiant heart within us. So when met with dogmatism or hate for your belief system or spirituality, simply respond with love. Use that as an opportunity to plant a seed.

At the start of my spiritual journey, I was met with rejection and extreme dogmatism. Fortunate for me, my family supported me and encouraged me to express myself. Others projected their fears and conditioning onto me, which disrupted my path and stunted my growth. Overtime, I realized everyone is operating from their own level of consciousness, or conditioning. When met with judgement, simply ask wisdom to speak through you.

Allah has created many routes to the path of love and enlightenment. There is not just one. It is perfectly fine to not fit popular narratives because what's for you is for you. Honor your truth, and don't allow anyone to shake your faith! We were all created to be our own expression of love.

Watch those hypocrites, and watch those parasites. Pure love is returning, and it is pure love that allows us to enter paradise.

In the chapters that follow, I place a heavy emphasis on the divinity within you, and the divine connection between our heart, womb, and mind. While engaging with this creative piece of mine, you will learn how to cultivate a loving relationship with yourself, and your pussy. Establishing a loving relationship with yourself, and with your sacred center can change your life. You will also begin the initial stages of your own self-healing and transformation. I aim to not only provide you with daily mantras but also encourage you to find true peace within your heart, mind, spirit, and womb.

Allow this book to help you channel your inner goddess and raise your vibration.

Sacred Instructions

Empress, the time has come for you to level yourself up. This short chapter is dedicated to providing you with a manual on how to use the yoni mantras effectively and how to maximize your results.

The format of this book will make it very easy for you to navigate. There are a total of 222 mantras divided into eleven chapters, with each chapter containing around twenty mantras related to the title and content of that specific chapter. At the conclusion of every chapter, there will be a sacred healing practice for you to complete. This healing practice can be completed during or after reciting the mantras, and each can be completed within the comfort of your own home.

Every goddess is on their own unique path to healing, and every experience will be different. Remember to trust in yourself and whichever higher power you call on to manifest all you desire. God, Allah, Mother Father God, Creator, whichever feels comfortable for you.

You do not need to be a woman to channel divine feminine energy. This book is not exclusively for women, but for women-identifying and nonbinary individuals as well. Divinity and sacred sensuality is an energy that is mutually inclusive to all.

To the goddesses who have undergone any surgery, procedure, or therapy that may have removed or altered your womb, please do not shy away from the contents of *Yoni Mantras*. This book was created for *all* women, and that includes you. If you have been diagnosed with any cervical or uterine cancer or have needed to remove your womb through a hysterectomy, your strength, courage, and spirit are truly admired.

Regardless of if your womb is present or not, the affirmations and practices of this book still apply to you, and your sacred center is still so powerful and divine. Speaking life into yourself, establishing a loving relationship with your sacred center, and caring for your yoni are always necessary. Allow the principles of *Yoni Mantras* to help bring you closer to your inner goddess and divine feminine.

How to Use Yoni Mantras

A mantra can be defined as a positive affirmation stated mentally or out loud during meditation or as a daily healing practice. When stating your mantras, it is vital that you have faith in what you are speaking. Without faith in your words, you will be wasting precious energy. The idea is to speak life into yourself and your womb. There is power in the words we say. Our words have the ability to manifest our deepest desires and assist us in attracting positive vibrations.

When you speak, your higher self can hear you, as well as Allah, the universe, and your sacred center. Speak your mantras in a soft tone, with an open mind and a receiving spirit.

There is no specific formula to using *Yoni Mantras*. The beautiful element of this book is that it is up to the reader's discretion to read the affirmations when and how they would like to. My recommendation is to find which chapters apply most to you and recite those mantras on a daily or weekly basis.

For the chapters that do not relate to you, dig deep to find out why they do not relate to you and how you can incorporate them into your sacred journey. Each chapter has a specific purpose and intention. If you are experiencing a disconnect with your yoni, open this book. If you are healing from past traumas or pain, open this book. If you are feeling happy and fulfilled, open this book. If you are wanting to manifest a dream, house, relationship, or the like, open this book.

As a goddess, you must understand the powers of speaking life into yourself. There is force and power in every word you speak, so it is vital to be mindful when using your words. The mantras of this book will assist you in reprogramming your subconscious mind to ultimately shift your reality. No matter where you are on your journey, there is always a lesson to learn.

Always remember to speak kind words to yourself and to others. Welcome to your transformation, Empress.

C H A P T E R

1

Empress Healing
& Inner Peace

The first chapter of Yoni Mantras is dedicated to cultivating true inner peace by deep healing all parts of ourselves because an empress deserves to live in peace. Our pussies are powerful, and very important to our anatomy and creation. However, our hearts and minds are even more powerful and sacred. Valuing your pussy is necessary, but always remember to value your soul, heart, and mind first. There is divinity within you.

Cultivating inner peace begins by truly getting to know yourself and innerstanding ALL aspects of yourself. The aspects of yourself you like, and the ones you don't like. True alchemy is acknowledging your imperfections, yet constantly evolving into the very best version of yourself. Your inner kingdom.

Always remember, the beauty on the outside of you is a reflection of the beauty within. By tending to my own inner garden, my soul essence began to relax and be at peace. I stopped looking for love outside of me, and felt the unconditional love of the Most High inside of me. More love, peace, and joy entered my heart space. The love I felt inside was so beautiful and radiant, nothing outside of me could disrupt my peace.

It felt as though I was a caterpillar who went into its cocoon to heal, release, and love on myself before blossoming into the beautiful butterfly Allah intended me to be. The true me. It was a very challenging time for me, but when you realize you're a diamond you'll see why life had to pressure you.

Heal yourself, to free yourself. Doctors, practitioners, pastors, and other "healers" cannot heal us the way we can heal ourselves. As an empress, you have the power to completely transform yourself. No prescription needed, just you. You were created to heal naturally. Remember, you are infinite.

Inner peace is a luxury that any human being can achieve. As we transition through the many phases of life, we are often presented with learning experiences, new energies, and new people, which allow us to grow on a consistent basis. If you consider where you are today versus where you were five years ago, you might smile and appreciate your goddess evolution.

As we grow, it is important to release and set free energy that no longer serves us. Once you make the decision to set yourself free from all unwanted or outdated energy, amazing things will happen.

Allah cannot bless us if we are still holding hands with an energy that no longer serves us. Heal yourself, to free yourself.

Pack Light

Healing may need to take place in the womb, mind, or heart. Erykah Badu once told us, "one day, all them bags gone get in yo way so, pack light". Stop reading and process this quote, auntie was putting us on game. Is your heart carrying heavy weight, or is it as light as a feather? Are you packing heavy or packing light? Ponder.

Packing heavy is holding onto the bad habits, toxic attachments, unresolved traumas, grudges, resentment, lack of self love, the list goes on. Packing light is finding forgiveness in your heart, not taking anything personally, attaching yourself to no thing, truly loving yourself, and living life freely and at peace.

It is time to shed burdens, insecurities, and the baggage that has likely taken up too much space blocking your heart from Allah's pure love. Free yourself!

Put the book down for a moment and give yourself a hug! Tell yourself how much you love yourself, and appreciate yourself. After all, Allah simply wants us to love ourselves, love others, and love our planet. Your heart is ready to give and receive pure love. Stay as light as a feather.

Love Your Inner Child

Most of our deepest wounds occur in our childhood. From birth to adolescence, we encounter so many phases, transitions, and experiences. A large number of us grow up in healthy settings, but a large number of us also grow up in dysfunctional families.

As young ladies, sometimes our innocence is robbed from us. This can show up as a parent who abandoned us, divorced/blended families, emotional abuse, physical or sexual abuse, or even an absence of love and nurturing. We each have our own story.

When we gain wounds so early in life, we are often not taught how to process the emotion or express ourselves. This in turn creates blockages in our sacral chakra, around our hearts, and births an unhealed inner child in all of us. The inner child truly never "grows up". She's always there, waiting to be acknowledged and cared for.

Anything you seek from other people is what the inner you is seeking from YOU. For example, a beautiful queen may go her whole life hoping to find true love. She may look for it through her friendships, relationships, or even acknowledgement at her job. What she's really looking for, is the love that's already inside of her. The pure love of the Most High.

When you truly love yourself, you are able to give and receive love from others. Learning to fully love yourself invites many blessings into your life.

Invest in a diary and begin pouring your heart onto paper. Think about how your childhood may have affected your adulthood. Were there wounds you were never allowed to heal from? Were there secrets you kept hidden and tucked away from the world? Do you feel that you received the proper nurturing you needed as a child? Write about childhood and adulthood experiences that brought you any form of hurt.

By journaling, you free your emotional body from baggage. Deep releasing and healing takes place when we allow our thoughts to flow onto paper. Also, by writing your thoughts, you are rewiring your subconscious mind. Most of our subconscious minds are full of shadows and buried emotions that we refuse to face, but we must.

Acknowledging your inner child will shift so much energy in your space. You will find that more peace, love, and happiness enters your space. Be loving to your inner child, be kind to her, tell her you love her. Write letters to her, write to yourself.

Listen to Yourself

One of Allah's greatest gifts to us is intuition. Intuition is the language of the soul. Your intuition is always speaking, so listen. It's that nudge you feel when you're driving a little two fast, or when you feel so comfortable and at peace in someone's presence. We can learn so much from our emotions!

Oftentimes, our inner peace is disrupted by feelings of fear, anxiousness, comparison, sadness and depression. These feelings arise because there is likely a part of us that is asking for acknowledgment and healing.

Spend time cultivating your own healing process. True inner peace is achievable for everyone! Tend to your inner child, learn from your lower and higher self, acknowledge your shadow side. Shadow work is important because it deals with your secrets, subconscious mind, and deep rooted insecurities.

Be loving to all parts of you. Allow any repressed emotions, unhealed emotional, physical, or sexual trauma to rise to the surface so that you can acknowledge them and heal from them. No need to relive the experience, but send loving energy to yourself if you were left rejected or unhealed.

Analyze Your Triggers

Pay attention to your triggers. Your triggers say a lot about what needs healing within you. Be mindful not to suppress your emotions. Suppressing the emotion, or running from it will only put a temporary patch over it. Get to the root of that emotion or trigger by writing in your diary, or seeking therapy. Express yourself and dissect how you feel. Feel the emotion, shift it, and elevate.

Be patient with yourself. Be gentle with yourself. Love yourself.

Below you will find journal prompts to create a foundation for your own introspection:

- In what ways do I judge myself?
- In what ways do my childhood wounds affect me as an adult?
- Is my womb carrying sexual/ancestral trauma?
- What are my triggers? Your triggers simply want love and attention from YOU.

True healing comes from knowing and loving all parts of yourself.

Does This Energy Belong to Me?

The more we evolve, the more a force in opposition to our ascension will come to attack or distract. When and if you ever feel a sudden dip in your energy, nightmares, feelings of anxiousness, or uncontrollable thoughts, perhaps there has been a breach in your auric field. Take a salt bath, say a prayer, and embrace YOUR energy. Do yourself a favor and return to a state of gratitude, love, & power. Activate your prana energy by taking 3 deep mindful breaths…

For my empathic empresses, be mindful of what energy is yours versus someone else's. Empaths and spiritually inclined individuals can pick up on outside energy very easily.

Your Auric Field

Every plant, animal, and human being has an auric field. Your auric field surrounds your body temple. It is a direct reflection of your current state of emotions, energy, and vibration. As human beings, when we vibrate on low levels of anger, guilt or shame, our auric field may be unhealthy or easily compromised. When we vibrate higher like Andre 3000 said, we are radiant, full of love, and glowing with magnetism.

During these times, it is essential to understand the realm in which we live in. We live amongst the seen, and the unseen, the living, the deceased, and high vibrational beings of love, or angels. Our auric fields sometimes carry energy from others, or from healthy/ unhealthy outside entities. Negative entities materialize as a result of our own internal weaknesses. This is why deep healing is so important.

Pay very close attention to your thought forms. You can tell what kind of energy or angel is surrounding you based on your thought forms and emotional state. Outside entities have the ability to communicate with us telepathically. This can cause confusion if we are not able to decipher what thoughts are our own, versus what thoughts are from outside entities. Are you creating negative scenarios consistently? Or are you thinking positive thoughts that inspire you and bring you peace?

Whenever you feel a breach in your auric field, call on your angels to handle that unwanted energy for you. Release it to your angels, cleanse your auric field and return to a state of gratitude, love, and joy. Not every battle is meant for you to fight. You are meant to live your best life, and grow as a soul.

My Herbal Salt Soaks are the perfect cleanse for your energy. After cleansing your aura, be sure to call back in positive energy by burning Palo Santo, or "holy wood". You can also draw back in positive energy by taking a rejuvenating spiritual bath full of rose petals, oat milk, essential oil, candles, and relaxing music.

Govern Your Own Mind

A lot of humans find themselves trapped in their mind, blocking their inner peace. The mind can be your worst enemy if you do not gain control of it, and strengthen it. When you find yourself over-thinking, check in with your energy and mindset. See the thought, acknowledge it, act on it or let it pass.

Think of yourself as being the sky, and each thought that passes are clouds simply passing by in the sky. This skill can be strengthened through meditation, reading books, and journaling. Simple activities that require focus. Spend an appropriate amount of time relaxing the mind, but also feeding it with soul food or sacred study.

Be mindful of what you consume as far as social media, music, and entrainment. Your subconscious mind has to process all that you consume. Your power lies in being the governor of your own mind.

The society we live in wants full control over your mind. We insert ourselves into different portals daily by scrolling through social media, watching TV, and basic entertainment. Be mindful that your brain is attempting to keep up with the timelines of the characters in the show, and your own personal timeline.

Find time to separate yourself and detox from heavy media consumption. You will find that over time, the anxiety and overthinking fades away and you can finally hear and create your own true thoughts.

As we grow and evolve, the brighter we shine. One of Allah's greatest gifts is that in every moment we can recreate ourselves. We can choose a negative thought, or a positive thought. Where our focus goes energy flows so protect your thoughts.

Always ensure to relax your energetic body, and your emotional body. Allow your mind to become a fertile pot for seeds of peace, love, and infinite possibilities!

Heart and Soul Alignment

The ultimate goal of deep healing is to achieve inner peace, and heart to soul alignment. We are all beautiful souls in this earth school. We are not here by happenstance! Life is a teacher to us. The good and bad experiences, the emotions, the lessons, the blessings are all here for the betterment of our heart and soul.

Our main mission in this lifetime is to experience life as a human being, to learn, grow, and ascend to new levels. By deep healing, we shift so much energy allowing more love and light to enter.

Our hearts are our most precious gem. When our hearts are light, our soul is at peace. When our soul is at peace, life truly transforms into our own personal heaven. As long as you are in alignment with your soul, which is committed to being your best and most authentic self, life is always conspiring in your favor.

The mantras on the following pages will assist you in manifesting deep healing and true inner peace. Remember, there will never be peace in your world if there is no peace within YOU. What does your inner kingdom look like?

Yoni Mantras

I accept my highest healing.

I am ready to heal all parts of myself.

As I heal myself, I heal the world.

It is safe for me to live in the moment.

I am fully at peace within my heart, mind, body, and spirit.

I give myself permission to release all that no longer serves me.

I forgive others, and I forgive myself.

I release any negative energy dwelling within my temple.

*I give myself permission to heal and welcome
unconditional love and compassion.*

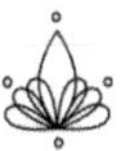

I am connected with the energy of Mother Earth.

I allow fresh energy to pour inside of me, and negative
energy be sent back to source and transmuted.

Loving energy surrounds me.

I have the power to heal myself.

I deserve to be free.

I am a constantly evolving goddess.

My temple is free of all abnormalities, impurities,
and imbalances. I am healthy.

I call all of my power back to me now.

I welcome inner peace into my life.

I clear my temple of any energy that is not serving my highest good.

I love myself unconditionally.

Sacred Healing Practice

Welcome to your first sacred healing practice, this is one of my absolute favorites. The amazing part about this practice is that it's beneficial for your womb, mind, body, and spirit. We all have a tendency of holding onto negative energy in all of our chakras. This, in turn, can cause blockages, and those blockages must be released.

Begin by showering first. Taking a shower before a salt bath is recommended as it rinses away any heavy energy. Water is a very healing essence, and it has the ability to assist us in releasing all unwanted energy. Water can be programmed simply by speaking intentions over it.

After your shower, run yourself a warm bath. Ensure the water is not too hot because you will get overheated and want to remove yourself from the bathtub after five minutes. If you would like to increase the effectiveness of this bath, feel free to look into my product line. My Herbal Salt Soak is formulated with healing herbs, combined with dead sea salt and himalayan salt. This combination would be an amazing addition to your healing practice. The bath soaks are amazing for cleansing your auric field, detoxing your skin and balancing your pH. Feel free to pair your cleanse with Florida Water, tea light candles, healing crystals, and your favorite music.

Connecting with the four elements while bathing will maximize your results considerably. The four elements are Air, Water, Fire, and Earth. You can use a feather for the element of air, your bath water for the element of water, a candle for the element of fire, and a crystal, seashell, or plant for the element of earth.

While submerged, take a second to remember what it is you need to set free. Think about what has been blocking your inner peace. Close your eyes and let the contents of your bath work pure magic on your skin, mind, aura and womb. After you come to a relaxed state, activate your prana energy by taking 3-5 deep breaths. Inhale faith, exhale fear. Inhale peace, exhale negativity.

As you soak your body, visualize all negative vibrations being removed from your mind, body, and spirit. What we visualize becomes our reality.

As your detox bath comes to a close, recite one concluding mantra while the water washes your unwanted energy down the drain.

I am grateful for you, but your time has served its purpose.
I see you, and I release you.

2

Embodying a Goddess and Your Femininity

In this chapter, I will be placing a heavy emphasis on your inner goddess and femininity. Yes, you are a goddess, and you are a divine feminine being. I find it safe to call myself "goddess" because after all, I am a daughter of the Most High. I am embodying the God-essence within me.

So, how do you refer to yourself? Do you call yourself a queen, a goddess, an empress, or nothing at all? Do you carry yourself like an empress? When you catch a glimpse of yourself in the mirror, are you in awe of how gorgeous you are? I want you to realize just how royal, beautiful, and divine you truly are. Take a moment to think about yourself. Think about your personality and all the attributes that make you who you are. There is no human being like you in this world.

You are unique and different in your own way. You are lightning, thunder, sunshine, and moonlight. You are a phenomenal woman, a queen, and an incredible human being. Your scent is so lovely, your skin is so soft, and you are sexy. You are magic. You are so valuable, so worthy, and deserving of all you desire. From this moment forward, I want you to walk, talk, live, and breathe like the beautiful being you are. Embody your soul essence and your femininity every single day so your vibrations will rise and you will attract your reflection.

Femininity

As a goddess, embodying your femininity is essential. Understand that femininity and feminism are two completely different concepts. Feminism places a heavy emphasis on women's rights and the equality of the sexes. Femininity, however, describes all of the behaviors, qualities, and attributes of a woman. Femininity describes the nature of the female sex and the degree of being feminine or womanly. Femininity is how you walk, speak, dance, carry yourself as a woman, engage with other people, or care for yourself and others, such as your man, your children, etc. The list goes on, but the key to remembering femininity is understanding your attributes as a divine woman.

Every person carries feminine and masculine energy. Usually, men possess more masculine energy, while women possess more feminine energy. Here are some examples of both feminine and masculine attributes for deeper understanding.

Feminine:

- Intuitive
- Stillness, Patience
- Emotional
- Soft
- Nurturing
- Empathic, Vulnerable
- Interdependent
- Sensual
- Gentle
- Submissive

Masculine:

- Logical, Rational
- Active and Adventurous
- Aggressive
- Provider, Protector
- Leader
- Strong, Assertive
- Independent
- Athletic
- Firm
- Dominant

Can you see the differences between the two? Every human possesses both feminine and masculine traits, but the idea is to find a healthy balance between the two. There is such a thing as being too feminine or too masculine.

In today's society, many women have lost touch with their femininity. Women are showing more aggressive traits, like *"What can you do for me?"* attitudes, and we tend to be heavily influenced by toxicity. In this day and age, it is very easy to lose touch with your femininity for many reasons. Our movies often portray women as more masculine than feminine, reality TV has convinced us that women argue with their men and other women every day, our female music artists have adopted a very masculine role, and the men in the music industry speak about women as if we are homies, hoes, or foes instead of soft feminine beings.

I heard a song recently, and the lyrics were low vibrational, degrading, and demeaning. All she rapped about was how she didn't need a man, had her own bag, felt above other women, had sex with men who were taken, and continued to glorify being a side piece instead of a queen to a king. Baby, I am here to tell you there is no value in this type of music. The more you listen to, watch, and speak about these unbalanced qualities, the more your subconscious mind will train you to believe you are less than and far from a goddess.

Our manifestations are often a reflection of what we consume. Be mindful of the music you listen to, the shows you watch, and the environments you put yourself in. It is very easy to slip away from your divine femininity when the music you listen to each day puts you down as a woman or speaks ill about you. It is okay to listen to music you enjoy, but switch it up sometimes. Everything should be done in moderation.

Remember, you are a reflection of what you consume, and you will attract similar energy. That is why I want every queen who reads *Yoni Mantras* to understand how sacred femininity is and how it should be treated as such.

Part of being a feminine woman is accepting love from others and giving it in return. We are often told to be "independent women," that we don't really need love and companionship. This totally false narrative was designed to divide the sexes, and many of us were not raised in environments where our parents shared a healthy relationship. It is perfectly fine to be independent and financially free, but being in love, sharing life with another person, and having genuine friendships or relationships are a part of the human experience. Our creator, Allah, designed us to value ourselves and share beautiful divine partnerships.

Be open to love, know that you deserve love, and the love you desire will be given to you in abundance. When there is a flow between feminine and masculine energy within a relationship, the dynamic can grow to be healthier and more balanced. The more feminine you are as a woman, the more masculine of a man you will attract. The reverse is true in that the more masculine you are as a woman, the more feminine men you will attract.

Every single day, play with your femininity. This does not require you to be girly, submissive, and super sweet all the time. Some days, you may want to express your femininity by being sweet and soft, while other days, you may want to be laid-back and mysterious. Both are completely acceptable, and you may discover things about yourself through expressing your femininity in different forms.

Femininity is not just about being kind, emitting a loving frequency, or playing with your feminine energy. It is also about enjoying your sensuality, your confidence as a woman, your softness, and your feminine attributes. You were blessed with a vagina, so you naturally have certain feminine features, characteristics, and traits within you. Channel those inner traits so you can reap the benefits of being a soft and divine goddess. Below, you will find a number of ways to channel your inner femininity.

- Allow your heart to speak.
- Connect with your sacred center, your womb.
- Take care of your body. Practice good hygiene.
- Moisturize your entire body.
- Smile and laugh more often.
- Compliment yourself, your friends, and your man.
- Dance to music. Move your body often and allow yourself to be free.
- Admire yourself in the mirror. Admire your naked body and your beautiful face.
- Straighten your posture. Sit, stand, and walk with your back straight and your chin up.
- Get out of your head and shift to your womb and heart more often.

- Give yourself permission to relax.

- Become more emotionally expressive.

- Spend less time on social media and more time in nature.

- Value yourself. Understand your value and your worth.

- Workout three to four times weekly. Be sure to practice yoga as well.

- Balance spending time alone, and with those you love.

- Explore your body.

- Wear perfume, makeup, or nail polish if you'd like.

- Limit toxicity and meditate often.

- Take excellent care of your temple.

- Love yourself, be your own expression of divinity!

Being feminine is not a hobby or a phase; it is a lifestyle. Practice being feminine every day, and you will see how your life will feel more balanced and fulfilling. It will not feel foreign or awkward for long because you will simply be returning to the natural-born goddess you always have been. Femininity is not for every woman, but the shift brings amazing rewards and peace. Be soft, be sweet, be humble, and be loving. *Yoni Mantras* will help assist you in becoming a divine, confident, and transformed woman, ultimately allowing all areas of your life to thrive.

Recite your mantras and speak them with true intention. Remember, the goal is to transform in totality and level up. The world is yours, Goddess; make the most of it and embrace your divine self.

Yoni Mantras

I am intelligently designed.

I am a beautiful, divine, and sensual goddess. I am magical.

All I need is within me now. I am complete.

I am radiating in my essence and igniting my inner femininity.

I am embodying my soul essence and embracing my femininity.

My masculine and feminine energies are perfectly balanced.

The beauty that surrounds me is also within me.

I am in love with myself. I cherish everything about
myself and embrace all of my imperfections.

I am perfectly crafted.

I am open to love, touch, and closeness.

I am a perpetual generator of positive energy.

I bathe myself in my feminine sensuality.
I am vibrating with love and light.

I am sexy, lovely, soft, and gorgeous.
Everything about me is beautiful.

I am at peace with my body. My body
was created to do amazing things.

My womb is a blessing.

I am a royal daughter, and I carry myself like a queen.

I am beautiful, powerful, and amazing. I am valuable and worthy.

I am at peace. I am blessed.

I am a creator, and a sweet and soft goddess.
Positive energy flows through me. I am a woman phenomenally.

I love myself so much. My confidence is constantly increasing.

Sacred Healing Practice

For this healing practice, we will be dedicating one full day to channeling our inner femininity. This practice will require you to spend time alone. If you have children and/or a husband, make arrangements to have one day and one night away to relax and rejuvenate. Book a hotel room, an Airbnb, or visit your local spa if you choose.

In this healing practice, you will complete a visualization meditation for your inner goddess to express herself and come to life. You'll want to make sure you activate all of your senses: sight, smell, hearing, taste, and touch. Your sensing organs allow for messages to be transferred to your brain. This will enhance your experience considerably.

Begin by playing relaxing and calming music, preferably with no lyrics so your mind can focus solely on your thoughts. Search for Zen music, or you may want to search for ocean waves or rainfall sounds. Indulge your senses by lighting a candle or incense while you run yourself a relaxing and rejuvenating bath. To enhance your self-love bath, add rose petals, essential oils, oat milk or oatmeal, healing crystals, and a scented candle.

You may want to have a glass of wine or a cup of hot tea to relax your entire body from the inside out. Remove your clothing and step into your bath. Make sure the water is just right for a long and rejuvenating soak.

The best way to connect with your inner goddess and femininity is to establish a relationship with her. Channel your inner goddess by getting creative and visualizing yourself as a divine being. She looks just like you, but is she glowing? Happy and smiling? Is she confident and embracing all of herself? How does she dance or move her body? How soft is her voice? Is she soft and graceful? Spend time admiring her and showing appreciation for her. This is your higher self, the best version of you.

After your relaxing bath is complete, rinse off and allow your body to air-dry, moisturize your skin, and get comfortable in your bed. You will now connect with your womb through yoni breathing and kegel exercises. This is a breathing technique consisting of inhaling and exhaling while you squeeze, hold, and release your pelvic floor muscles in rhythm with your breath.

Yoni breathing is designed to awaken your womb, enhance your womb connection, release womb blockages, tighten the pelvic floor muscles, and increase relaxation, sexual energy, and oxygen in the bloodstream.

Yoni Breathing Technique

Step 1: Inhale deeply for four counts while squeezing your pelvic floor muscles. These are the exact same muscles you feel when you have to pee.

Step 2: Hold this position for another four counts while you visualize healing energy surrounding your womb. You may want to visualize this as a white or pink light.

Step 3: Exhale for four counts and release your pelvic floor muscles while visualizing your womb and full body releasing all tension and toxicity. Repeat steps 1 through 3 until you feel relaxed and relieved.

After connecting with your womb and higher self, allow your mind to be free and clear. Lay back and release all of your muscles and allow your body to be totally relaxed. While on your one-day vacation, be sure to spend time in nature, hug trees, feed yourself your favorite foods, limit your media interaction, and give yourself permission to embrace an upcoming transformation.

Feel free to join me for a deep restorative and meditative retreat. During my Jewel Retreats, relaxation and restoration will be our top priority. You will be fed, nurtured, catered to, and poured a glass of wine, if you'd like. Not only will we focus on meditation and relaxation, I will also show you how to move your body through lap and pole dances, slow dances, and yoga. It would be a pleasure to meet and guide you through your feminine transformation.

If you are unable to travel, you are welcome to join me virtually for sound baths, meditations, and online dance classes. Visit my website at www.yonimuse.com or connect with me on instagram @theyonimuse for upcoming retreats and virtual healing sessions.

3

Establishing a Relationship with Your Yoni

When a gardener wants her garden to be fruitful and beautiful, she will continuously water her plants, talk to them, touch them, and nurture them. In return, her garden will blossom into the most gorgeous roses, lilies, fruits, and vegetables. She may decide to eat her fruits and vegetables, place her flowers on display, or simply allow her garden to flourish for years on end. This gardener will be able to enjoy the fruits of her labor simply because she established a loving and caring relationship with her sacred garden. Your heart, mind, body, spirit, and womb are no different from a garden. Each sacred center deserves a caring, loving, and fruitful relationship.

Establishing a relationship with your yoni is like establishing a relationship with yourself. As goddesses, we must ensure we treat our bodies like a garden. Watering, feeding, loving, and caring for ourselves is fundamental and always necessary. If you want to see balance in your life, relationships, and higher self, you must cater to your heart and womb space. Your pussy deserves to be cared for, loved, and spoken to on a regular basis. Keep your pussy healthy, and your heart as light as a feather.

Have you ever considered that your womb has been with you since the day you were born? For some women, the womb cleanses and detoxes twelve times a year through her menses. Your womb gives life to your children or unborn children. Your womb is your husband's safe place. Your womb is your most sacred center that provides you with your pussy power, creativity, passion, and pleasure.

While establishing a relationship with your yoni, it is important to have an open, receptive mind. My yoni spoke back to me thirty minutes after speaking with her for the first time. Yes, she spoke back. Conversing with your yoni is never a one-sided conversation. She can hear you and will respond if necessary. You can ask your womb for clarity, creativity, and healing—all of which she will provide for you. She will speak back to you, so listen to your pussy.

My First Conversation with My Womb

It was late at night, and I had just finished reading *Sacred Woman* by Queen Afua, which encouraged me to connect with my sacred center. I encourage every woman to read it as well. Honestly, I did not take it too seriously when I first read it. I found myself having thoughts like, *How is my womb going to talk back to me?* I had some reservations, but I decided to give it a try because why not? So I rubbed my hands together to generate heat and applied them to my pelvis, right where my womb is. I had no idea what I was doing; I just did it. I said the following words:

My precious Yoni,
Thank you so much for all that you do.
I am forever grateful for you.
You have been with me since the very beginning.
I apologize for being absent for so long, but
I am here now.
Thank you for providing me with my intuition.
Thank you for naturally cleansing me.
Thank you for keeping me healthy and nurturing me.
Thank you for being my future husband's safe place.
Thank you for being my future unborn child's home.
You are a gift.
Show me what I need to do to care for you.
Show me what you want more of.
Show me what you want less of.
How can I make you happy?

If my memory serves me correctly, those were my words verbatim. I said each sentence with intention, and I set an intention to hear back from her. I was open to hearing or feeling whatever she needed me to.

Now, one thing every woman needs to understand is when you have a conversation with your womb, you are expressing that you are one hundred percent open to hearing what she has to say. You must be open, even if you are not ready for an honest and unexpected response. For this reason, you must understand that you cannot get upset or mad when she converses back with you. Sometimes, it may be a response you don't expect.

Thirty minutes after speaking with my yoni, I was relaxing, watching a movie. I felt myself getting a little sleepy, so I decided to shut my laptop down and get ready for bed. I don't know about you, but I have no problem pleasuring myself. It's safe, fun, and a great way to explore your body with no risk of getting pregnant.

Once in bed, I reached over for my toy and turned it on. Tell me why it *died* on site—no light, no power, no vibration. It literally died. I laughed so hard and said, *There is no way…hmm. Let me put it on the charger; maybe it needs to be charged.* I placed it on top of its charger and returned to my movie.

Some time passed before I thought, *OK, let's try this again!* I grabbed it from the charger, turned it on, and nothing happened. My toy *died* died. No, it didn't need to be charged; it didn't get wet or anything like that. It just died. I laugh about it now because, looking back, I was so shocked that my little toy had just called it quits on me, but it also took about five minutes for me to realize that I had just asked my womb to "show me what you want less of."

Crazy, right? Could it just be a coincidence? How ironic is it that my longtime friend decided to stop working the very night I spoke with my sacred center. I didn't understand. My powerful womb had a force so strong, it discontinued the power of my vibrator. Wow! Truthfully, I had to dig deeper to find out exactly why that happened.

After careful reflection, I realized maybe I needed to use my sexual energy for other purposes. Maybe instead of self-pleasing right before bed, I needed to meditate or say affirmations. Maybe I needed to stop watching pornography. I will never know exactly why my toy died that night, but I will say a lot of great things have come from that sacrifice. I reflected a lot more on my sensual and sexual energies, and I used that time before bed to meditate, pray, read, or converse with her again. I made it a whole month before buying another one, but that's a story for a different book!

My purpose of telling this story is so each woman who decides to connect with their womb on this level can know that as long as you are open to hearing from your higher self, you will be provided with an answer. Every. Single. Time. Your experience will likely be different from mine. You may actually hear a voice with a random but well-needed message. Who knows? I will not know, and you will not know until you speak to her.

On the following pages, you will find twenty mantras dedicated to establishing a relationship with your womb. Feel free to read the mantras weekly, or you can read one per day. However you choose to say your affirmations is completely fine; there is no right or wrong. Remember to say them with intention, believe in your words, and be open to receiving.

Yoni Mantras

My pussy is a precious jewel.

My sweet and precious womb, I am initiating a relationship with you because I need you. You are precious to me, and I will continue to protect you.

I trust my womb's choice.

I love you. I have always loved you.

My pussy is a sacred portal.

I am open to receiving your guidance, blessings, and nurturing.

I have intimacy intelligence.

My womb connection has always been a solid
one, and it will continue to flourish.

She is me, and I am her. You are me, and I am you.

If my womb is out of balance, my life forces are also out of
balance. I am restoring power and balance within my yoni, so
I can receive clarity mentally, emotionally, and spiritually.

Talk to me, Yoni. Tell me what you are feeling. Show me what you are feeling. Show me how I can please you better.

I trust that all answers I need are within me.

I love my yoni. My pussy is sacred.

I give my womb permission to speak freely and openly. I trust in my womb to communicate my best interests and my most true intentions.

Yoni, reveal to me what you want more of and what you want less of. Show me how I can make you happy.

My womb is a vital part of my temple.

I am forever grateful for my healthy womb. She continues
to nurture me and keep my body cleansed of all impurities.

I am establishing a strong connection with my feminine creative energy.

Yoni, talk to me. I am open to receiving.

I am so grateful for your existence. I love you
so much. Thank you for loving me.

Sacred Healing Practice

Goddess, you made it through this vital chapter. You have looked over your mantras, recited them, and spoke with true intention. Blessings are underway! It is now time for your sacred healing practice. Using the mantras on the previous pages, you will complete a healing ritual that will help maximize your results. This ritual will not require any tools or equipment.

Lay on your back in your bed with both eyes closed. You want to be facing the ceiling. Keep your full body in alignment, ensuring your body faces the sky. Now, rub your hands together to generate heat. Once you feel your hands are warm enough, place them over your womb. Your womb is located at the base of your pelvis by your lower belly.

Now that you have your hands placed over your womb, begin having your conversation with her. It may feel weird at first, but trust the process. It is recommended that you speak out loud, but if your privacy is limited, you can say them quietly or in a whisper. Tell your womb you love her and are grateful for her. Send love her way through your mind. Use your imagination to picture your womb filled with love, happiness, and joy. Use your mind to send healing vibrations to her as well. Don't forget to ask her for guidance, healing, and intuition. Ask her to provide you with clarity. Lastly, tell her once again that you love her and are grateful for her.

Feel free to use my prayer during my first yoni conversation as inspiration. Conclude your prayer and remember to be open to receiving.

4

Show Appreciation for Her

Whenever we show gratitude for someone or something, we receive more love, wealth, and abundance. Gratefulness is the key to growth, manifestations, and happiness. When you are not showing appreciation for the things you have, it is easy for the universe to take it away from you. This is the principle of "taking something for granted."

For every human being, it is important to be grateful and appreciative in this lifetime. Every day, before your feet touch the floor, you should express gratitude for your life, health, family, and all positive things in your life. One thought of appreciation creates another and another. Before you know it, you'll put yourself in a great mood by analyzing how blessed you truly are.

Now, let's discuss the reasons why we should show appreciation for our wombs as well. Every vagina has benefits!

- The vagina is self-cleansing; however, the vulva is not.
- The vagina naturally repels dirt and debris.
- The vagina has the ability to fight off mild infections on its own and can restore its own natural pH if treated properly.
- The vagina naturally lubricates itself.
- Your vagina is a fountain of good health. Eating clean pussy can provide amazing probiotic benefits for your lover.
- Your womb cleanses itself twelve times a year through your menses.
- Your womb creates life.
- Your womb can house and nourish a child for nine months.
- Your womb can give birth to a whole human being.
- Your womb provides you with your femininity and creativity.
- Your yoni can experience multiple orgasms at one time.
- Your yoni is your partner's safe place.
- When paired with the right person's penis, toy, tongue, clit, or finger, your yoni can help you experience immense pleasure.

With this extensive list of benefits, how have we never expressed appreciation for her? As a goddess, it is important to show appreciation for her so she can continue to be magical.

Your Monthly Cycle

Your nipples are sore, you're bloated and cramping, and your skin is breaking out. It's about that time! Your cycle is underway.

When these symptoms arise, it is easy to become annoyed or frustrated because, now, you have to make sure you have all the necessary products and comfortable clothing for your cycle. You may also have to apply a heating pad to your tummy to relieve your cramps. What a hassle, right? Your period can be emotionally and physically draining, but let's dissect exactly what your period is.

Every month, your ovaries release one of your precious eggs. Once this egg drops, it waits to be fertilized by sperm. If your precious egg is not fertilized within your fertile window, your uterus begins the process of menstruation. During menstruation, your body naturally eliminates the lining of your uterus and your unfertilized egg. The cramps you feel stem from contractions of the uterine lining or your womb. The contractions help expel the lining and pass it through your body. No matter how inconvenient your cycle may seem, embrace that your body is naturally doing what it needs to do to keep you healthy. Show appreciation for your healthy reproductive system. During those three to five days, you are given a chance to renew, release, and revive. A natural detox is taking place.

*Full Disclosure: I am a huge advocate for natural and herbal remedies. I do not advise the consumption of man-made pills; however, always talk with your doctor before taking any tips or advice from me or any other person. Everyone's body is different.

There are a number of women who are currently not experiencing their monthly cycle. This can be caused by birth control or being overweight, underweight, or in menopause, and other various reasons. If you are on birth control, I recommend seeking alternative contraceptive methods. Birth control may cause imbalances within your womb and disrupt the natural hormonal exchange. Ask your doctor about the long-term effects of birth control with regards to fertility and the possible withdrawal symptoms once you decide to stop taking it. There are many other ways to practice safe sex without conception, and those should be explored first before taking man-made medications daily.

There are various reasons why a woman may want or require birth control. Often, they are not given a choice, or it is simply her preference, which is fine. However, if you are wanting to avoid pregnancy, try tracking your period and fertile window each month with period tracking apps. There are only a few days out of each month where a woman is fertile. Although tracking your fertile days is not guaranteed to prevent pregnancy, it will eliminate the need for man-made contraception, including the Plan B pill.

If you are taking birth control for menstrual regulation, PMS, endometriosis, or PCOS, do not discontinue use without talking to your doctor. You may also want to try holistic methods, or by using your natural healing abilities to heal yourself as well. Speak life into your womb daily, ensure to keep her cleansed, steamed, and healthy. Yoni Steams can be found on my product line at www.yonimuse.com.

Lastly, never give your monthly cycle a negative name. Embrace her and know that your period truly is a blessing.

Below, I have provided a few natural tips for your monthly period:

- Instead of taking a man-made pain pill for your cramps, try applying a heating pad to your tummy. I also turn my vibrator on and rub it over my tummy to relieve my cramps as well.
- Ask your womb to remove your period cramps, back pain, and breast pain.
- Work out or practice yoga while on your period. Getting active will help alleviate your menstrual pain.
- Try to stay away from eating spicy foods during your cycle, as they increase the intensity of cramps.
- Try to use natural pads instead of tampons. Tampons can cause small lacerations on the vaginal wall. Besides, you want to allow your blood to flow right out of your vagina.
- A high intake of animal products may cause a heavier cycle. The more you eat foods that bleed, the more you will bleed. This includes dairy products, chicken, cow, turkey, and all other foods that walk, fly, swim, or crawl.
- Although period sex is not advised, orgasming while on your period will also help period pains. Sex on your period can bond you to the other person. So unless you're wanting to bind yourself to a person, refrain from period sex. Use your favorite toy instead!

- Using my Goddess Body Oil, give yourself a womb massage or have your partner rub the outside of your sacred center.

Empress, give thanks to your lovely lotus flower right now. Thank her for all of her magical capabilities and for keeping you healthy as you grow. Send loving energy to your womb while you recite the following mantras.

Yoni Mantras

Womb, thank you so much for cleansing my uterus twelve
times a year. I will not take my cycle for granted.

Thank you, Yoni. You are absolutely amazing and so
magical. Thank you for doing exactly what my body needs
you to do without being asked. My period is a blessing.

My uterine lining is releasing as it should to prepare
my womb for a new, healthy, and perfect cycle.

My womb is a blessing.

My feminine instincts are activated.

Thank you for being my husband's safe place. He will
forever feel at home as long as he is inside of you.

I heal my womb, and my womb heals me.

I am thankful for my womb's many benefits.
I am blessed to be born with a vagina.

My monthly menses is a great blessing. My menses helps
me honor my spiritual, emotional, sexual, and energetic needs.
I will no longer resent and devalue my sacred cycle.

Yoni, I am so appreciative of your essence.
You are an important part of me.

I am beyond appreciative of the creative power within me.

Womb, I acknowledge and appreciate you for having unconditional love for me. Although I have allowed undeserving men to enter you and doctors to drug you, I appreciate that you are still here with me. You are strong; therefore, I am strong.

I appreciate the phases of my menses and embrace the blessings it brings.

I trust in my womb to provide me with my deepest intuition and confidence within myself.

Yoni, you naturally cleanse me. For that, I am so appreciative of you.

I trust my womb choice. I trust myself.

Womb, you are a dynamic force.

The relationship I share with my womb is strong and unbreakable.

Yoni, I will continue to honor you and treat you with love and care.

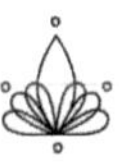

My reproductive organs are healthy, and I am grateful.

Sacred Healing Practice

If you've ever gotten a massage, you know how amazing it feels to be caressed with warm oil and healing hands. As you leave the massage parlor, you likely feel so relieved, relaxed, and rejuvenated. It is an amazing feeling. In this healing practice, you will be giving yourself a womb massage. This massage will provide many benefits for your womb. You can give yourself a womb massage sitting, lying down, or standing. I like to play music, but if you'd like to massage yourself in silence, that is also perfectly fine. Feel free to use a lightly scented lotion or my healing and rejuvenating Goddess Body Oil. Just to be clear, this massage will be external, not internal. This is not a masturbation exercise.

Using both of your hands, feel below your belly and a bit above your pubic hair where your womb is located. Use your hands to create a diamond shape and apply a little pressure to that area with your fingertips. Move your hands in circular motions on your womb. Continue to do this throughout your womb massage while sending loving energy her way. This massage is the perfect way to thank your womb because this is good for her. The massage not only heals her and makes her feel good, but it also allows more blood to circulate around your lotus flower.

This is a practice that should be conducted at least once a week to maintain optimal vaginal health. Speak to her while you caress her with your healing hands. Recite your mantras and visualize your womb being filled with warmth, vitality, health, and increased blood flow.

5

Confidence in Your Yoni

With this chapter, I intend to provide you with a guide on how to embrace your pussy. After all, it belongs to you and only you, so do not be afraid to fully embrace it; learn to love it. Confidence of any kind starts in the mind. You must silence the voice in your head that tells you you're not pretty, you cannot start your own business, or you will never get married. Once you silence that voice, your positive thoughts can speak louder. Confidence is absolutely necessary as a divine feminine woman. Once you have true confidence in yourself, the world is yours.

The yoni is a very sacred, precious, and powerful gem. In this day and age, women everywhere are insecure about their vaginas. Society has taught us that a vagina should look a certain way to be beautiful. We have seen this ridiculous standard spread from social media pictures to memes to pornography, and even via someone else's mouth.

I want each and every queen reading this book to understand that your yoni is flawless. Vaginas come in all shapes and sizes, and it is perfectly OK if you feel that yours looks different. Chances are there are plenty of women who feel the exact same way you do. It's OK.

Your vagina does not need to be "perfect." Regardless of if you have a long or short labia, skin discoloration, ingrown hairs or hair bumps, uneven vagina lips, or any other "imperfection," your yoni is perfect and normal. My product line includes a healing Pussy Bawm and Pussy Scrub that can be used for minor impurities surrounding your yoni, including ingrown hairs, razor bumps, discoloration, and more. My bawm is herb infused and can also be used as a treatment for hsv outbreaks or a pussy polish before sexy time.

Do not allow this demanding society to tell you what your lady parts should look like, and do not allow another person to tell you your lady parts are not beautiful.

No vagina looks and smells perfect. Every pussy has a slight scent! Some have the fragrance of herbs, while others are simply the natural body aroma. Believe me when I tell you that men appreciate when a pussy has a healthy scent. You should not feel self conscious unless you are releasing a foul odor similar to fish, trash, or anything else unpleasant.

A natural clear/white discharge is also healthy and normal. Your yoni is self cleansing, so it is perfectly normal to see small traces of vaginal secretions in your panties after a long day. It is advised that you see your OBGYN if the discharge is clumpy, foul smelling, or odd colors such as green, yellow, or brown.

If you choose to shave your pussy, cool. If you don't, that's cool too! It is YOUR pussy. Do with it what you please. Besides, if hair was meant to grow there, it is safe to leave it be. If you do decide to refrain from waxing or shaving, be sure to keep your pubic hairs trimmed. Bacteria, moisture, and debris can trap itself within pubic hair causing an unpleasant odor so be mindful of your cleanliness.

If you are insecure before getting intimate with someone, let those worries go right here and now. Embrace your yoni and know that the person who is meant to love you will not disrespect or judge any physical flaw you think you have. There is beauty in imperfection, so know that your vagina is beautiful, wet, tight, juicy, and flawless.

Recite the following mantras and speak with true intention. Your yoni deserves to be embraced.

Yoni Mantras

I fully embrace my beautiful vagina.

My yoni is my most precious jewel and my most delicate flower.

My vagina is flawless.

My pussy is beautiful and lovely, just like the rest of my body.

My vagina does not need to satisfy modern-day standards.
My imperfections are all normal and beautiful.

My pussy is healthy and vibrant.

My yoni is sweet like honey.

My pussy is worthy of love, and so am I.

My yoni is beautiful. My yoni is precious. My yoni is exquisite.

I will not allow others to dictate what I should look like.

My vulva is a sacred art.

I give myself the best because I deserve the best.
The love I have for myself is unconditional.

My yoni is centered, grounded, and pure.
My yoni is sacred, and so am I.

There is peace within my sacred center. I am in
balance with my yoni's natural rhythm.

My yoni is beautiful in every way.

I will not compare my yoni to others'. My yoni is different and unique in its own way. I love every aspect of myself.

Yoni, I love you, and I embrace all of you.

Yoni, you are beautiful. Thank you for being a part of me.

I release all insecurities. I welcome confidence, comfort, and self-esteem.

Yoni, you are beautiful. Yoni, you are healthy. Yoni, you are precious. Yoni, you are sacred.

Sacred Healing Practice

This healing practice will require you to step outside of your comfort zone. Some women may have no problem completing this practice, while others may find it difficult. No matter where you are in your journey, this practice is designed to bring you closer to your sacred center. Release all inhibitions and allow yourself to be vulnerable while on this journey.

Take a handheld mirror or sit in front of any mirror in your room. Remove your bottoms and panties. Spread your legs and take a good look at your yoni. Spend time admiring your vulva. Your vulva includes your labia, clitoris, urethra, and the entrance to your sacred center. She's so pretty, isn't she? She belongs to you. She is yours. The vagina is truly a beautiful element of the female anatomy. Consider how grateful you are for the many benefits she provides for you. Smile at her. Compliment her.

Continue this practice on a regular basis to connect with yourself and your yoni. Do this for your womb health but also for your self-esteem. Recite your mantras while completing this practice to enhance the experience.

C H A P T E R

6

Pleasure and Sensuality

As an empress, you deserve to feel pleasure. You also deserve pure love and high vibrational sex. This chapter and chapter one were my absolute favorite to write. I'm blushing just thinking about it! Haha. Regardless of if you are sexually active or not, this chapter is applicable to all women. I want this to be a safe place for you to read about intimacy, sex, and sensuality. As a feminine woman, it is your divine right to give and receive pleasure and embrace your sensuality.

Allah created sex to be a sacred energy exchange between you and your divine partner. When the divine masculine merges with the divine feminine, pure love is radiated.

Pleasure may come in the form of exchanging energy through kissing, touching, rubbing, grinding, or bouncing. Oh my goodness, see? I am already getting ahead of myself! But seriously, you deserve to reach your peaks and feel the most pure form of love.

I will be writing this segment from a heterosexual perspective. For this reason, I will be referring to your partner as a man. However, if you are homosexual or bisexual, feel free to simply replace all of the heterosexual notations with whatever fits you best. Love is love, and I support it all.

Sensuality

noun; the enjoyment, expression, or pursuit of
physical—especially sexual—pleasure

Feminine energy is so powerful. The ability of a soul to express sensuality through a physical body is amazing. One of the best ways to get in touch with your sensuality is to explore your body, your natural flow of movement, your nakedness, and all things relating to your divine feminine essence. You have the right to explore your sensuality in any way that pleases you.

We are taught to suppress our sensuality and sexuality. However, both elements are exactly why we are here today. Sex is truly sacred because of its role in cultivating peak experiences of love, oneness, and healing. Why shouldn't we embrace our sensual nature? Why shouldn't we take time to indulge our senses?

During your sacred healing practice, you will be exploring each of these elements, and I encourage you to complete the practice at least once a week. Release all of your inhibitions and allow your inner goddess to come alive. I want you to walk, talk, dance, and live like the goddess you are.

Through enhancing our sensuality, we are not only getting in touch with our femininity, we are also increasing our sexual confidence. Once you increase your sensuality and sexual confidence, you can enjoy intimacy and pleasure more deeply than you ever have.

Take a moment to rub one of your pressure points. You have pressure points all over your body, but let's start off with the pressure point in the very center of your forehead at your pineal gland, or "third eye." Use your finger to rub this pressure point in a circular motion. Does that feel nice? Does it feel stimulating to you? Yes? That is because your body and spirit love being touched, caressed, kissed, spanked—you get the idea!

Pleasure

Your womb is your sacred portal, the entrance to your yoniverse. She has the ability to provide you with immense pleasure and very little restrictions. The best part about having a vagina is being able to have multiple orgasms at one time and still being able to keep going. Men require a little downtime and recovery before they can jump back in the game.

There are so many women who have no idea what it feels like to orgasm! Most of us do not know how to achieve one, and a lot of men do not know how to give one. I am here to enlighten you. An orgasm feels so amazing to your sacred yoni. It is as if your walls contract with pleasure, you ooze your sweet juice, and a rush of energy flows through your body. When you reach your peak, it is one of the most inexplicable feelings you will experience sexually.

You can achieve an orgasm internally, via your g-spot, or externally, via your clitoris. To achieve an internal orgasm, your partner (or yourself) must be able to locate your g-spot. Your g-spot is located inside of your vagina, right behind your clitoris. Essentially, your partner has to stroke this spot multiple times and just right for you to reach your peak. Do not allow a man to simply jerk off inside of you; make sure you get yours, too, babe. His strokes may feel nice during the moment, but sex was not intended to only provide orgasms to men. It requires a little bit of work and patience, but once it happens, you'll want one every single time—as you should.

As mentioned before, you can also achieve an orgasm externally, through clitoral stimulation. There are more than 8,000 nerve endings in the tip of your clitoris alone. Men have half of that in their penis. A clitoral orgasm can be achieved through a man tasting your lotus flower, playing with it with his fingers, or by using different toys, such as a vibrator.

If you've never used a vibrator on your clitoris, I recommend you try it because it may be an amazing experience for you. If you are already familiar, then you know exactly what I am talking about! If you are opposed to masturbation, ask your partner to use it on you. Your partner can stroke you while he plays with your clitoris. Your yoni wants you to explore her as often as you would like.

When you reach your peak, it will feel as though an abundant amount of energy is flowing through your body. Your yoni will ooze your sweet juice, your walls will contract with pleasure, and your full body will return to a relaxed state. To achieve an orgasm is such a beautiful and pleasurable experience. I invite all of the empresses that read this book to experience an internal and external orgasm.

Wet Pussy Tips

Our bodies are so intelligently designed that once we are aroused, our brain signals to our yoni that is time for sex. The biggest fear most women have is to lose their vaginal wetness during sex, or at some point in their lifetime. Though getting "dry coochie" is annoying, sometimes that is simply our yoni telling us that something is wrong, or that she is not feeling your sex partner. Your pussy talks, so listen.

There are many tips I can provide for you to prepare your yoni for sexual intercourse. Below you will find a few ways to avoid dry coochie:

- Drink half your body weight in ounces per day
- Have sex with a king you genuinely love and care for. Sex feels totally different when you truly appreciate your partner.
- Consume womb teas, formulating for your pussy's optimal health
- A diet high in fruits and vegetables will keep your pussy healthy and naturally lubricated
- Pineapple Juice and Cranberry Juice are excellent drink choices the week of your dick appointment.
- Know your body! He cannot please you if you are unsure how to please yourself.

- Foreplay is essential! Let that man take his time with you before he enters your yoni-verse.

- Give your pussy time to warm up. Never go straight into it without building at least a little anticipation

- Get out of your head. Oftentimes, we cannot get wet or orgasm because we are too caught consumed with thoughts. Live in the moment baby, you deserve that.

- Speak up. If he does not pleasure you, let him know. Do not be afraid to hurt egos.

- Invest in an herbal vaginal oil. Never be afraid to use a natural lubrication. Your pussy might appreciate that very much.

- Steam your pussy! Yoni Steams can be found on my product line at www.yonimuse.com.

Healthy Sex Tip

Before getting intimate with any person, always be aware of their STD status, as well as your own. Regardless of if a condom is used, this is absolutely essential. This will allow both sexual partners to make an informed decision before proceeding with intimacy. In addition, always pee after sex and wash yourself to reduce the chances of bacteria buildup and infection.

Recite the mantras on the following pages, and remember, you are a divine sensual and sexual being who deserves pleasure. You are a goddess, a queen, and a very sexy woman. Yes, you are.

Yoni Mantras

I deserve all the pleasure. I am worthy of being loved. I will receive pure love only.

My body is rightfully mine, and I choose to do with it whatever I please.

My man must take his time with me, for I am gentle and graceful.

I refuse to let an undeserving man inside of my sacred center.

Yoni, you deserve pleasure. If he does not please you, speak up. You deserve to reach your peaks, contract with pleasure, and ooze your sweet juice.

I am a sensual goddess. I admire my body,
my femininity, and my divinity.

I will only allow a man to enter my yoni-verse if he has
proven he is worthy of having such a precious diamond.

I am embracing my sexuality and sensuality.

My yoni is a delicate flower.

I am not ashamed of my sensuality.
My sensuality is a life force flowing through me.

My yoni is healthy and balanced.

I love admiring my naked body and my beautiful face.

I am not embarrassed or ashamed to pleasure my yoni.

My sexual energy must be honored and protected.

My womb is open and ready to receive the
energy of love. I radiate this essence.

I release all inhibitions and insecurities. I give my yoni permission to orgasm with my deserving lover. I will no longer hold back. I will release myself and become more in tune with my sexual energies.

My womb is perfectly balanced and able to receive multiple orgasms.

My yoni deserves gentle, sweet, and soft love.

My heart, mind, soul, and yoni will align to create divine sensual experiences in my love life.

I feel pleasure and abundance with every sacred energy exchange I experience.

Sexual pleasure is a beautiful gift I deserve to receive.

Sacred Healing Practice

This sacred healing practice will likely come naturally to most women. I understand some women are very comfortable with dancing, while others may feel awkward or disconnected. This is perfectly fine because there is a first time for everything. This sacred practice will require you to dance, strip, move, wind, and explore your body. You may want to do this in a very private setting, and I recommend doing this often.

Put on your favorite slow song. It can be R&B, reggae, afrobeat, or any song you love. It should be one that sends chills down your spine or makes you feel sexy. My selection is "One Night Only" by Sonder. My body reacts differently to Brent Faiyaz, haha.

Now, stand in front of a full-length mirror if possible. While the song plays, slowly remove your clothes as sensually and sexily as you can. If you are not yet comfortable with being naked in front of a mirror, it is OK to wear panties and a T-shirt. Wine your body to the sound and beat of your chosen song. Pay attention to how you sway your hips because this is stimulating your yoni and allowing blood flow to penetrate her and relax her from within.

Use your hands to caress your naked body. Start in your hair, then move them to your neck, down to your breasts, your tummy, and your booty. Watch yourself. Admire how beautiful and sexy you are. Really pay attention to how nice your hands feel against your soft skin. Smile at yourself! This is an excellent way to increase confidence as well. Do this often, and you will see a difference in your sexual, sensual, and body confidence.

Remember, the beauty that is outside of you is a reflection of the beauty within you.

7

Yoni Healing and Womb Wellness

In this day and time, there are so many factors that can contribute to illnesses, cancers, imbalances, and diseases within the body and the womb. Disease can be created through our food intake, water supply, environment, sexual partners, toxic feminine products, stress, and many other factors. Our temples are so precious and sacred, it is vital that we feed ourselves wholesome and electrifying foods, and limit our stress levels. By being mindful of our consumption, we save ourselves from complications later in life.

Eating healthy is good for your overall well being, and your pum pum. There are many women who suffer from cervical cancer, infections, cysts, fibroids, heavy menstrual cycles, tumors, infertility, and sexually transmitted diseases. If you are sexually active or consume animal products, you should detox your vagina on a regular basis. A healthy alkaline diet can dramatically change your overall health.

Before we proceed, I want to state that I am not a gynecologist, medical practitioner, or licensed nutritionist. I can only advise and inform you based on what I have learned and experienced. Results are not guaranteed, and individual results may vary.

The Power of Food Intake

Your doctor probably won't recommend rest, meditation, time in nature, and diet adjustments when you become sick. In fact, they may prescribe a man-made pill or a procedure that will likely cost thousands. That is why it is up to us to take care of our own health and womb wellness so we can hopefully avoid unnatural remedies. As a goddess, it is important you feed your temple wholesome foods, herbs, and clean water. It is no secret that the foods we grew up eating are the same foods that allow diseases and cancers to run in our bloodline. Our parents and grandparents spent the majority of their lives eating meat, dairy products, sodas, potato chips, sugary candies and drinks, and massive amounts of gluten. All of the foods listed above do not serve your body in any capacity. In fact, they deteriorate your insides and cause you to crave more, gain weight, lower your vibration, and increase your chances of acquiring diseases or cancers.

To create a disease-free environment, one must consume mostly alkaline fruits, vegetables, whole grains, nuts, seeds, and herbs that are filled with vitamins and minerals. Your drink choices might also need adjusting. Although sugary drinks taste yummy, it is important to consider the high amounts of sugar, chemicals, and preservatives that exist within those drinks. In addition to this, our water supply is heavily contaminated with fluoride, flushed prescription drugs, and other toxins. Look into your county water supply before you continue to drink tap water. If you love eating meat, don't stop because I say so. Conduct your own research, but be sure to consume it in moderation.

Change your eating habits and your thought processes, and your body will return to a more healthy, alkaline state. I grow my own food so that I know exactly what I am putting into my body, and where it came from. I speak to my plants, and speak intentions over my food as well. Mother Earth is abundant and provides us with all that we need!

Emotional and Mental Factors

Our food intake is not the only factor that affects our bodies significantly. When we hold on to stress, worries, fear, ancestral trauma, or toxicity, acid is created within the body. Holding onto these negative energies is a direct result of internalizing our feelings. Excess acid in the body sets the foundation for disease. Diseases in the womb include painful or heavy periods, tumors, fibroids, cysts, illnesses, and imbalances. Diseases beyond the womb include colds, flu, high blood pressure, cancers, and other abnormalities. One of the main causes of disease is increased acidity in the body. Be mindful that if you are internalizing an abundance of negative energy, you are unknowingly creating a space for disease to flourish. Release it all. I want you to take your power back and heal yourself by eliminating stress and all unwanted energy. Refer to Chapter 1 to learn exactly how to heal and free yourself.

Sex and Acid Dick

Goddess, you've likely never heard this before, but acid dick is a real thing. I want you to value your womb so much that you refuse sex from a man who is highly acidic. If your partner consumes high volumes of alcohol, drugs, animal products, and processed foods, chances are he is highly acidic and so is his sperm. If you are allowing him to cum inside of you on a regular basis, know that his acidic sperm is having an effect on your womb, emotions, and pH.

The same is true if he is not a divine person. We become who we have sex with. That is how powerful sex truly is. Sex to me is a sacred energy exchange, so if you are having sex with someone who is negative or carries a negative vibration, those elements can be passed to you through sexual intercourse. Some men vibrate on extremely low levels, causing them to be the perfect host for outside entities. To put simply, men can transfer their demons onto you and vice versa. Sexually transmitted demons are real, and a lot of men are looking for a beautiful divine queen to "put his weight on" so be careful honey.

Really get to know a man before you allow him to enter your sacred portal. As an added bonus, you can ask him to take a salt bath or smudge him before intercourse just in case.

If you ever finish having sex with a man and feel drained,

confused, or irritated, that is a sign that the energy exchange was toxic. After allowing a man to enter your yoni, you should feel relaxed, uplifted, and pleased. Your sexual partner should know how to send loving frequencies to your full body while inside of you.

Value your body temple and only make love to a king who is divine, deserving, and free of negative vibrations. Treat your womb like your most precious jewel.

Yoni Healing

If you have the power to bring relief to a child's scraped knee or soothe your honey's soreness after a long day of work, why wouldn't you be able to apply that same energy to yourself?

If you are cramping during your cycle, feeling depressed or ill, or simply lacking energy, you have the ability to reverse that feeling. Whenever my body is experiencing painful cramps, I put my hands over my womb and ask that the pain be removed immediately. I continue to speak life into myself until the cramps fade away. It never fails. No matter what imbalance or illness you are experiencing. If your yoni is not operating at its maximum capacity right now, use your healing hands, prayer, and intention to restore her.

All you need to do is use your mind, words, and imagination to restore your health and release the imbalance. Talk to yourself, pray to yourself, and tell yourself you are feeling better. Once the mind declares what it wants, the body follows suit. Your mind controls everything.

The mantras on the following pages can also be used for your breasts or any other part of your sacred temple.

Yoni Mantras

My womb will always and forever be healthy,
disease-free, and clear of all negative energy.

My yoni is pure.

I am calm. I am peaceful. I am happy. I am stress-free.

My womb cleanses itself daily to protect me from
infections and abnormalities. My yoni is healthy.

I release even the slightest imbalance right now.

I release all the pain I may be carrying within my sacred center.

I release all pain, stress, and emotions that may
have a negative effect on my womb's health.

Any pain previously experienced has been lifted
and removed from my sacred center.

As I place my hands over my womb, I lift and
remove all impurities that may reside within me. I
am releasing all things that no longer serve me.

Yoni, you are healthy. Yoni, you are pure. Yoni, you are free.

I am free of all tumors, cysts, and fibroids that may dwell within me.

My yoni naturally lubricates and cleanses itself.

Oxygen, energy, and blood easily circulate through my temple.

I have the ability to heal myself. I have the divine
power to restore health and vibrancy to my womb.

My yoni is perfectly balanced.

My womb is in a natural healing process. I trust
her to restore balance and health within my body.

My womb is healthy; my womb is free.

Loving energy surrounds my womb.
My reproductive system is fully functioning.

I feel healed because I am healed.

I release all imbalances from my sacred
center. Release, release, release...

Sacred Healing Practice

This healing practice will be similar to the one you completed during the first chapter in that it requires you to spend a day channeling your inner femininity. I never recommend douching for a vaginal detox. Douching causes an imbalance in our pH levels, and it also allows unnecessary chemicals to enter our womb space. This is not the way to detox your lotus flower. This sacred practice is great for routine detoxing, relaxation, or right before your annual checkup.

Take your yoni on a vacation. Visit the park, the beach, or any place where you can relax with Mother Nature. Put on a dress or a skirt with no panties. You want to ensure your yoni is open and free when releasing all abnormalities.

While at the park, in the bath, your bedroom, or any place of your choosing, find a comfortable position, either lying down or sitting up. Spread your legs slightly, warm your hands, and place them over your yoni. You want to ensure your legs stay open during this practice, so all unwanted energies or diseases can be released into the water or air while you pray. Really tune in and focus on your rejuvenation. Inhale, imagine the fresh air pouring inside you like water, and release any disease or imbalance on your exhale. Allow nature to nurture your yoni.

Give your yoni permission to release. Do this for as long as you please or until you feel free. Recite the following sentences or your affirmations.

I release all unwanted energy.
I release any abnormality or disease within my womb.
I release any fibroids, tumors, or cysts within me.
I release all impurities within my womb.
My womb is free from toxicity.
My womb is healthy.
My womb is free.
I welcome health, love, and abundance.
I welcome a healthy womb.
I welcome a disease-free yoni.
Ase, and so it shall be.

8

Attracting Peace, Love, and Positive Vibrations

In the previous chapters, we discussed the importance of detoxing your womb, mind, life, and spirit. We also discussed how to release negative energy from within and care for your mental health. In this chapter, we are welcoming growth and discussing how to attract positive vibrations to replace negative energy.

As noted before, detoxing your womb, body, and mind is absolutely essential. As you navigate through life, you will realize how we naturally experience positive and negative situations. Sometimes the negative situations can weigh heavily on our spirits, and that is why detoxing and releasing is important. We must welcome all experiences the divine pushes our way because they help us flourish and grow stronger.

Embracing and attracting are just as important as detoxing. To truly enjoy our lives, we must learn how to align with our divine self and attract the vibrations we deeply desire. A positive vibration is anything that brings you joy or peace, including wealth, health, love, abundance, freedom, happiness, and more. The list could go on and on because there are so many beautiful elements to life we all can enjoy if we learn how to attract them. To attract positive vibrations, you must understand your reflection, practice gratitude, be open to giving, and align with your higher self.

Understanding Your Reflection

You are a reflection of what you attract. This is a very important statement I want you to always remember. If you find you are attracting friends who are kind, smart, and extroverted, chances are you are also kind, smart, and extroverted. If you find you are attracting spiritual men who have achieved higher consciousness, you are most likely spiritual yourself. We are always attracting the reflection of ourselves. It is a beautiful thing because once you align with your higher self, you will find that people with positive vibrations easily enter your life and have a great impact. You will also have an impact on them, which is wonderful.

Attracting your reflection is not always a good thing. Oftentimes, we find ourselves in bad situations over and over again. This causes frustration for us because we want better but can't seem to find it or achieve it. The good news is bad situations have a way of serving us. We experience both positive and negative vibrations so we can learn and elevate. For example, if a woman finds she is constantly meeting men who are insecure, overprotective, or toxic, she is likely lacking self-love, confidence, and awareness of her negative patterns. If this queen wants to attract a man who is confident within himself and not toxic, she must align with her higher self. This may include finding confidence within herself, realizing her true worth, and increasing her self-value. If you find that an undesirable situation is taking place in your life time after time, try to consider what that situation is trying to teach you. Once you learn that lesson, the test will be completed, and you will level yourself up. Remember, you are a reflection of what you attract.

High vibrational energy attracts high vibrational energy. Low vibrational energy attracts low vibrational energy.

The Act of Giving

One of the best ways to attract a desire is to give that exact desire back to the world. When you bless someone else, the divine recognize your generosity and return the favor back to you. The important thing to remember is to give and expect nothing in return. Have faith that when you bless someone, your efforts and generosity will be rewarded. If you want to attract love, give love! Use your arms to embrace your friends and family. Kiss your close family members on the forehead and cheeks whenever you can. Smile at a stranger you pass in the store. Give a compliment to your coworker. Become a person who is constantly giving and showing love, and the universe will return love in abundance.

The same principle is true with money. If you want to attract more money, give money. Offer to pay for your friend's meal when the two of you go out together. Donate to a locally owned small business. Find an honest charity to donate to. Tip your waitress. Give your spare dollars to the homeless. This same principle may sound familiar because it is taught to members of the Christian faith. Christian leaders advise their members to give 10 percent of their earnings to the church, and God will return the favor in abundance. The same principle applies to those of any religious or spiritual belief. No matter who you give to or how much, you will be blessed in return.

Focusing on Your Frequency

There are many things we do as humans that cause us to create blockages in our lives. These blockages then result in fewer blessings, slow manifestations, and a lowered frequency. To attract the blessings you want, you need to focus on your frequency and the energy you are putting out into this world. If you are releasing negative energy into the universe, you will be given that same energy in return. If you wake up in the morning and think, *Damn, I have to go to work*, you are already starting your day off on the wrong foot. Instead, express gratitude and appreciation for your job and say, *I am blessed to have a job*. You cannot expect to attract good energy if you're giving off negative energy every day. Gossiping about others, preying on the downfall of others, and expressing jealousy are also ways to create blockages and limit what you attract.

You also want to be mindful of your thoughts. Your thoughts

have a huge impact on your frequency. Change the tone of your thoughts from boring, repetitive, and negative to happy, affirming, and positive. If you find yourself having one bad thought after another, change that narrative and think a happy thought. For example, instead of thinking, *I'll never find someone who's perfect for me,* think *The man who was created for me is on his way to me now, and I cannot wait to bless him with all of my love.* See how easy that is? Watch what happens when you replace negative thoughts with positive perspectives.

Lastly, try every single day to align with your higher self. In my mind, I think of my higher self as a strong, successful, beautiful, and impactful goddess of the universe. My higher self is who I aim to be every single day. She is the best version of me. Consider this: Five years ago, you were nowhere near the queen you are today. You have blossomed into a lovely flower, and that is something to smile about. Although you've grown so much, there is always room for improvement. You want to ensure your thoughts, actions, words, and relationships align with those of your higher being. Once you put together a picture of your best self, you will be able to work toward being that person. Show the universe that you are ready and able to receive all you desire, and you will be blessed in abundance.

Speak the following mantras on a daily basis. Say them with true belief and intention. I cannot wait to hear all about your growth!

Yoni Mantras

I am attracting all I desire.

I am valuable. I am worthy. I am beyond blessed.

I am following my intuition. Allah is always conspiring in my favor.

I trust that all of my needs are met. I am unlimited.

Money gravitates toward me. I am receiving wealth and abundance every day. Money flows to me easily and continuously.

I am attracting love, happiness, wealth, and prosperity.

It is safe for me to live in the present moment.

I am free.

Everything I need and want is being supplied
to me. I am open to receiving.

I am attracting genuine friendships and relationships.
I am blessed and happy to share my life with others.

I am living in harmony. I am in alignment with my higher self.

I am attracting tremendous wealth. I am
creating multiple streams of income.

My heart, mind, body, and spirit are free from toxicity and
negativity. I am ready and available to receive all of my blessings.

I appreciate all of the abundance in my life.
I am grateful for what I already have.

Positive vibrations gravitate toward me.

I am happy to give and open to receive. I trust
that my generosity will be reciprocated.

I am connecting deeply with my higher self
and am raising my frequency.

I am attracting healthy relationships, increased income,
unlimited manifestations, and true happiness.

My womb is attracting a worthy and valuable king.

I am worthy of a luxurious life.

Sacred Healing Practice

This healing practice should be conducted on a regular basis. If you can, try to implement it into your schedule at least three times a week. You should start by smudging your place with a sage bundle. Smudging your sacred space clears the energy field of all energy. When smudging your place, be sure to open your windows so all energy can escape into the outside atmosphere. Smudging does not need to take place three times a week unless your home or car has frequent visitors or you are trying to release old toxic energy or memories. Palo Santo, or "holy wood" is an excellent tool to welcome positive energy after clearing the space.

Once your place is smudged, turn on some music and grab your pen and pad. During this sacred practice, I like to listen to Erykah Badu, Sade, or Jill Scott. With your pen and pad, I want you to write down two things. Start off with writing down everything you want to attract into your life. Use the list below for inspiration. Your list may look similar to mine, or it may be totally different. But whatever your values are, be sure to write them down.

I want to attract:

- Increased self love, and inner peace
- Genuine and fulfilling relationships
- Business and new streams of income
- Wealth and abundance

- A loving and loyal partner
- Positive vibrations and happiness

This list is extremely short but only serves to show you some ideas of how to generate your list. For your second list, I want you to focus on your higher self. What does she look like to you? What is her personality like? What are her values? Your higher self already exists; you just have to discover her, nurture her, and align with her. Your higher self is simply the best version of yourself. My personal list can be found below.

The Goddess within me is:

- Sweet, feminine, and caring
- Rich as hell and a magnet for wealth
- Beautiful and Highly Vibrational
- Perfectly balanced
- Ambitious and Determined
- Intuitive and Spiritual
- In tune with nature

Once both of your lists are drafted, meditate and visualize all that you claimed. The best way to piece everything together is to visualize yourself having and doing all you desire. Close your eyes and meditate with your journal. Read your lists aloud, and speak of each element as if it has already been given to you.

As a bonus tip, sleep with your manifestation journal under your pillow to maximize your results!

9

Fertility and Preparing for Conception

This chapter is specifically dedicated to the women who are preparing to conceive a child or are experiencing complications with conception or miscarriages. Before I go any further, I must make a few careful statements. Each and every woman's experience with fertility and conception is different, and results may vary. I am not a doctor, doula, gynecologist, or obstetrician, so I cannot guarantee you'll see results from using the mantras and healing practices.

This chapter simply serves as a safe space where one can speak lovingly and positively to their womb. As mentioned before, results may vary, as each woman's reproductive system is on its own unique healing path. Regardless of where you are in your journey, speak life into your womb and never give up on the power of miracles. The key is to speak with intention and truly believe in your words and the divine power.

Causes of Infertility

There are many factors that contribute to conception complications. Some can be cured, while others require assistance from medical professionals. If you are experiencing complications with conceiving a child, I recommend visiting a medical professional to first find out exactly what the root cause is. Once you find out what the root cause is you can adjust your affirmations to directly match your unique healing process. Infertility can be caused by one or multiple reasons listed below:

- Fallopian tube blockages
- Pelvic Inflammatory Disease (PID)
- Bacterial infections
- Multiple abortions
- Recurring and untreated infections
- Trauma
- Endometriosis
- Male infertility
- Uterine infection
- Uterine abnormality
- Hormone imbalance
- Irregular menstruation

Please stay on top of your annual exams, as an untreated sexually transmitted disease (STD) or infection can permanently damage your reproductive organs. Unsurprisingly, women are not the only ones who experience fertility complications; men are also capable of experiencing these issues. This is especially true for men who consume toxic foods and high amounts of alcohol and drugs, live a sedentary lifestyle, or have allowed an STD or infection to go untreated for a long period of time. Do not doubt yourself or your reproductive system before finding out exactly what's causing your fertility issue.

There are a number of ways to boost your fertility and prepare for conception naturally, including:

- Avoiding alcohol and high-caffeinated beverages
- Exercising
- Taking your vitamins (You should look for vitamins with folic acid.)
- Eating organic and wholesome foods
- Practicing yoga and relaxation exercises
- Having your partner massage your tummy or womb
- Conducting your own womb massage
- Looking into healing herbal remedies
- Avoiding sugar and artificial sweeteners
- Consuming healthy fats, such as nuts, seeds, and avocados
- Speaking lovingly to your womb

I never want you to give up on having a child. No matter where you are in your journey, maintain a positive and optimistic mentality about your desires. Speak life into yourself every single day, meditate

on your desires, visualize yourself with your baby, consume wholesome foods, remove toxicity, and never give up!

The following mantras are applicable whether you are preparing
to conceive or are having complications. To increase the effectiveness
of the mantras, state the mantras with your lover. Two people meditating on one desire doubles the manifestation power.

Yoni Mantras

My womb is in a healing process. When the moment
is right, I will carry my own child inside of me.

My ovaries, follicles, and womb are fully healthy and nourished.

I carry healthy babies in my womb. My babies will thrive
in their mother's womb. I give life through my womb.

My ovaries and uterus are in perfect harmony.

My womb is open to receive the perfect embryo.

My birth was a blessing to this world. My womb
will provide blessings for this world as well.

Blood, oxygen, and energy easily circulate
through my reproductive organs.

I am on my path to conception.

My body is perfectly designed.

I invite a baby into my womb. I am ready
to conceive and give birth to life.

My womb is ready to receive a healthy baby.

I have the ability to heal myself from all imbalances within my womb.
I release any womb blockages that may be present inside of me.

I am fruitful.

I trust in my womb's divine power to conceive.
I trust in you; I have faith in you.

My womb is a healthy vessel for my unborn children.

I am excited to create life inside of me.
Thank you, Womb, for this blessing.

My womb holds healthy ovaries that are
pink, warm, nourished, and healthy.

My partner releases healthy sperm.

I am fertile and so is my partner.

Every day, I give thanks because I am one
step closer to meeting my unborn baby.

Sacred Healing Practice

If you've ever looked into the Law of Attraction, you may know a little about the power of manifesting through our thoughts, words, actions, and visualizations. What we create in our minds, we can create in our reality. That is the way the divine power works. What you speak, write down, act upon, or visualize every day can be granted to you as long as you believe. In this healing practice, you will be conducting your own womb massage and visualization.

This practice can be done with my Goddess Body Oil or your favorite massage oil or lotion. This practice will be done externally. Warm your hands, locate your womb (right under your tummy and above your pubic hairline), and rub your womb in circular motions to stimulate blood flow. This is healthy for any goddess, whether you are trying to conceive or simply want to revive your womb. Apply pressure to your sacred center and send loving, healing energy her way.

While massaging your womb, I want you to visualize yourself in the early stages of pregnancy. With your eyes closed, imagine yourself taking a pregnancy test in your bathroom. Visualize yourself reading a positive confirmation that you are pregnant! Take a deep breath and smile. How does it feel to you? Are you crying tears of joy? Are you jumping up and down in excitement? Do not let go of this imagery. I want you to also visualize your tummy growing with life inside. Imagine feeling your unborn baby's small kicks on your belly or hearing your baby's light snores late in the night. Continue the visualization by imagining the very moment when your doctor places your baby on your chest. You look deep into your baby's eyes and kiss their cheek for the first time. It is real; it is happening! Smile during your imagination, and recite your mantras to increase the effectiveness of this practice. Do this consistently. Although it may be hard at times to "make believe," keep pushing through. Show the divine power how much you desire your angel and believe that, soon, it will be given to you and your partner.

I cannot wait to hear your success story, and allow me to congratulate you in advance on your bundle of joy!

10

Healthy Pregnancy Mantras

If you've flipped to this chapter, chances are you are preparing to have a baby or you have already found out you are expecting a bundle of joy. You may even be a few months into your pregnancy, or you may be days away from your due date. No matter where you are in your pregnancy, I am ecstatic for you, and I want to congratulate you on your blessing! If you are not pregnant yet and are still in the process of conceiving, you may also find this chapter useful. The mantras will help you manifest your pregnancy and your healthy baby as well. You are even free to participate in the sacred healing chapter with your partner, as two people meditating on one thing increases the speed of the manifestation.

There are many things to consider after you first find out you are expecting a child. When a woman finds out she is pregnant, she will likely experience a wave of emotions. She may be happy, ecstatic, relieved, shocked, and every emotion in between. You probably have had thoughts about the changes in your body, childbirth, growing closer to your partner, finances, or any other aspect that comes with having a baby. Although these things are important to consider, I want your main focus to be your baby's health and your womb wellness. You ultimately want to ensure your womb is healthy so your baby can be healthy as well.

Before you read this chapter's nutrition and pregnancy tips, please consult with your obstetrician or primary care physician about your diet and pregnancy care. I am not a doctor, doula, gynecologist, or obstetrician, so I cannot guarantee you'll see results from using the mantras and healing practices.

Pregnancy and Nutrition

As you may already know, I do not recommend the consumption of meat, animal products, or toxic foods and drinks. When carrying your baby, you want to ensure you're feeding yourself healthy, nourishing, and nutrient-rich foods, so your baby can develop into a healthy and active fetus. Below, you will find a short list of foods that may assist you in nourishing your baby.

- Fruits and vegetables are essential during your pregnancy and after you give birth as well. Vegetables are rich in antioxidants and fiber. Try to consume leafy greens, such as kale, spinach, and broccoli, as well as nutritious fruits, such as mangos, berries, plums, beets, and avocados.

- Consume a high intake of water. Water flushes the body and is a beverage that does not contain high amounts of sugars, carbs, or GMOs. If you can, try to consume water that is filtered, as tap water can be detrimental to your body over time.
- Legumes are an excellent source of plant-based folate, calcium, fiber, protein, and iron. Legumes include lentils, peas, beans, and chickpeas.
- Foods high in folate are essential for the health of you and your fetus. Without folate, your precious baby may become more prone to disease and infections later on in their lifetime.
- Whole grains are also important during your pregnancy, as they contain high amounts of fiber, magnesium, and protein. Look for oats, quinoa, and other whole grain foods that satisfy your taste buds.
- The most important food elements or supplements you want to look for are fiber, calcium, zinc, iron, folate, folic acid, and vitamin D.

In addition to ensuring you are consuming a healthy diet, you also want to be mindful of your physical and emotional well-being. Your precious baby can feel when their mommy is happy, sad, stressed, or tired. When you feel your body getting to a point of exhaustion, make sure you allocate time to rest, recover, and rejuvenate. Keep your stress levels low and try to maintain a positive mindset and energy throughout your pregnancy. Maintaining your fitness and body strength is very possible while carrying your baby. Prenatal yoga is an effective exercise for maintaining a healthy pregnancy. Not only does it relax your body, but it also alleviates discomfort, pain, indigestion, and stress while strengthening your posture and pelvic floor.

While taking care of your body, you also want to develop a relationship with your unborn baby. Connecting with your baby during pregnancy enhances the bond between you and your baby when they're finally born. Although your bundle of joy has not been delivered yet, you can still develop a loving relationship with your baby, so when the two of you finally meet, he or she will feel comfortable and happy knowing your voice, your words, and your energy. Below, you will find practices you can do by yourself or with your partner to connect to your baby.

- Rub shea butter or my Goddess Body Oil on your belly every night and send loving energy to your baby.
- Get active with your baby. It is perfectly fine to practice light exercises during your pregnancy, and it is also normal to maintain a regular sex life.
- Read to your baby as often as you can. Hold the book in front of your belly and read aloud so your baby can hear you and be entertained by you.

- Have your partner kiss your belly as often as he can. Kissing sends loving energy to both you and baby. You'll want your partner to kiss your belly for the baby and your forehead for you.

- Speak loving words to your baby. Tell your baby how much you love them and how much you cannot wait to watch them grow up. Speak loving words with a soft voice to your precious baby.

- Take a relaxing bath with your belly. Allow the water to fully cover your belly. Sit back, relax, close your eyes, and think about your baby.

- Play music or sing to your baby. Soft sounds and slow R&B are lovely and will soothe your baby.

- Respond to your baby's kicks. Gently push against the baby, rub your belly where you felt movement, or simply say, *"I feel you, baby."*

- Your partner can also partake in bonding activities. Ask your partner or your other children to bond with the baby by speaking, singing, or reading to them. Kiss, hug, and love on your fetus as much as possible.

- Use my Goddess Body Oil to conduct a womb massage on your belly. Be soft and gentle when massaging your womb and tummy. This stimulates blood flow to your belly and reproductive organs, and it also provides substantial benefits to your skin.

- After your baby is born, ensure you breastfeed him/her. Your breast milk is nutrient-rich and allows your baby to grow strong and healthy. Try to breastfeed as long as you can before utilizing baby formula.

Lastly, recite your mantras to your baby. This can be done with or without your partner. I encourage you to recite your mantras on a daily basis to encourage a healthy baby and a healthy womb.

Yoni Mantras

I am happy, blessed, and thankful to be carrying a healthy baby. I will have a healthy and peaceful pregnancy.

I will only allow positive thoughts and energy to flow through my mind, heart, and body.

I am accepting of my pregnancy experience. I welcome all changes to my body because I know my baby requires assistance from my natural abilities.

My baby knows all is well.

My womb is nourishing, nurturing, and providing a healthy space for my unborn baby.

I will give birth to a perfectly balanced and healthy child. My
body is designed to nourish, protect, and grow my baby inside of me.

I welcome the changes in my body, and my womb
is perfectly equipped for a successful delivery.

I am healthy, able, and fully capable of giving
birth easily. I am a strong woman.

My baby is being provided with all of the nutrients
they need to be healthy, able, and nourished. They
will be born healthy and at the perfect time.

My baby is perfectly positioned at all times.

My womb is free from toxicity, imbalances, and abnormalities. My baby is safe and healthy.

I release all pain that may be present within my body. My back, belly, feet, and organs are free from swelling and pain.

My body is in perfect harmony. My womb is balanced and providing my baby with a nourishing and loving home.

My baby is free from diseases, illness, abnormalities, and impurities. I love my healthy baby.

I love my partner, and my partner loves me and our baby.

I will use my voice to express what I need and what I am
not comfortable with during my pregnancy and delivery.

My baby is in the perfect position to be born into
the world with ease, comfort, and peace.

My precious baby will be a blessing. My baby will
strengthen the relationship I have with my partner.

I will have a successful delivery, and my baby will
be blessed with optimal health and balance.

I love my baby so much. My baby is a
blessing to me, my family, and this world.

Sacred Healing Practice

No matter how far along you are in your pregnancy, I urge you to practice this exercise with your partner. It is important to send loving and thankful energy to your womb during your pregnancy. Your womb is nourishing and providing a safe home for your unborn baby, so it is important to recognize and show appreciation for your womb's amazing abilities.

Sit or lay down, and ask your partner to lay very close to your tummy, where your baby eats, sleeps, and grows. Have your man rub your tummy with or without oil, and say these words (or similar) to your womb:

Thank you, Yoni. Thank you for carrying my healthy child.
Thank you for providing my baby with all of the
nutrients, vitamins, and water he/she requires.
Please continue to keep my baby safe and away from harm.
Please continue to nourish my son (or daughter).
Please continue to grow with my baby and protect him/her.

Have your man kiss your womb, your tummy, then your forehead and repeat, *"Thank you, Yoni."*

11

Manifest Your Desires

The final chapter of *Yoni Mantras* will be the ultimate and most powerful lesson: manifestation. This transition includes recognizing the power within you and understanding how to use this power to transform your entire being.

There are so many divine elements of life that a lot of people have absolutely no clue about. Many of us have lost touch with our higher selves, our ability to manifest, and the divine powers within us. People commonly underestimate just how powerful we truly are, and this is because we have been programmed to think, speak, and act a certain way. The people who govern us do not want us to achieve a higher consciousness because, then, the impossible will become possible. There will be far less stagnancy and illness and fewer brainwashed individuals. However, more and more people are starting to recognize just how powerful we are as human beings. We truly are divine beings, and we all possess infinite power.

We are all children of the Most High, birthed from the union of Allah and Mother Earth. We are made from nature, but the essence within each of us is GOD. I am intelligently designed, you are intelligently designed, and our planet is intelligently designed. We were created to be our own expression of love, to co-create our own beautiful reality.

You are not your body, your skin, or your physical features. Your body temple is simply a vessel this lifetime, a temporary living space. Know that there is divinity within you. A part of you that is forever, your God essence, your soul essence. The Kingdom of God is within you. (Luke 17:21)

If we were made in his image, then call us by our name. We truly are gods and goddesses with amnesia. Alhamdulillah because most of us are waking up and remembering who we are. As a collective, most of us are achieving higher levels of consciousness, tapping into our higher selves, and embodying our divinity!

As a divine being, you have unlimited power at your disposal. There is also the divine power assisting and guiding you on your journey. You may refer to this power as God, Allah, the Infinite, the Universe, etc. With the assistance of the divine, your angels, ancestors, and your higher self, you have the power to live your life in a higher consciousness and manifest all you truly desire.

This is a realm of free will. We choose our thoughts, we create our future. Remember, you are a co-creator. While it is perfectly fine to manifest material desires such as houses, cars, and financial wealth, remember that manifesting inner peace, healing, and balance is equally as important. My very first manifestation was inner peace within my heart, mind, temple, and yoni. I achieved that manifestation and now I teach it to others, what a blessing.

Don't become so immersed in feeding your flesh that you neglect your spirit. We were born to make manifest the glory of God that is within us first, then create our own beautiful life second.

The Law of Attraction

If you are unfamiliar with the Law of Attraction and Universal Laws, I suggest you study each concept and get acquainted. One of the best and most powerful ways to manifest a desire is to write it down. Something magical happens when you put pen to paper and write out exactly what you want in this lifetime. You can write down qualities you want in your partner, business goals and aspirations, monetary desires, travel plans, and everything else in between. Once you write your goal or post it on your vision board, you are officially declaring your desire. Allah, the universe, and the powerful forces that be will then work to bestow that blessing upon you.

Tip: Keep a small journal of all of your dreams, goals, and aspirations. Read it often and sleep with it close by or under your pillow.

Meditation and Visualization

Another powerful way to manifest your dreams or desires is to meditate on them. Your thoughts become your physical reality.

If you can see it in your mind, you can achieve it in your reality. Practicing meditation is not only good for manifestation, but it is also great for calming the mind, gaining clarity, and relaxing the body. When you meditate, focus heavily on exactly what it is you want to manifest, and do not spend time thinking about anything opposite of that. See it, feel it, hear it, and smile because it is on the horizon. Visualize yourself doing, being, or having what it is you desire. Where are you? What kind of business do you own? What kind of house are you living in? What countries, cities, and islands are you traveling to? Visualize yourself in those spaces and feel every emotion you would feel as if it has already taken place. By imagining your desire in your mind (4D), you will then be able to manifest it in the physical world (3D).

Adjust Your Mindset

A lot of people have this idea that you must *have* something to *do* something, so you can *be* someone. For example, one might say, *"I need money to open my own business, so I can become a wealthy and free person."* This mentality should be adjusted to *Be. Do. Have.* One must first *be* the person they aspire to be, so they can *do* what they were called to do and *have* the things they desire. Remember this principle and never forget it. The first step to manifestation is to become. Become a reflection of your higher self and your divinity. The universe will recognize your actions and provide you with the tools, resources, connections, and insight you need to elevate to the next level. Trust in your process.

Manifesting through Orgasm

Pay close attention to what I am about to say and please have an open mind because it's a little freaky! There is a such thing as manifestation through orgasm. So many positive forces and energies are flowing through our bodies when we climax. Energy is racing through our bodies during that very moment. I want you to try this alone or with your partner. When you feel yourself reaching your climax during sex or masturbation, focus heavily on your deepest desires or dream. I know it's easier said than done because the feeling of an orgasm is far too explosive to think about business, love, traveling, or big purchases, but I want you to try it.

You can also do this for your lover. If you know there is something he desires, manifest that reality for him through his orgasm. When he reaches his peak, focus all of your energy on that job he wants or that home he wants to build for you. Send him or yourself all of your loving energy while the two of you climax together. With practice and belief, miracles will happen.

Gratitude and Appreciation

When manifesting, you want to always show gratitude and appreciation. When you wake up in the morning, give thanks for your life, health, job, home, and mobility. Whether you are pushing through a storm or feeling on top of the world, give thanks for where you are. Give thanks to Allah for assisting you in creating the life you want to live. Give thanks for the positive and negative experiences that have helped shape you into the person you are today. Always be thankful, and live your life as if you have already been blessed with your deepest desires.

Make A Move

In addition to these principles of manifesting, it's important to note you will not go anywhere if all you do is pray for movement. You will not manifest anything if all you do is think about it. Manifesting requires action. Faith without work is dead. How can Allah create opportunities for you if you are not putting in the grind? Write that business plan, book that trip, open that investment account. Plan your work, and work your plan. Even if it is a baby step or a small gesture, you must act. Staring up the steps will get you nowhere. You have to actually take a step to move forward. Do your part so Allah can do his.

Lastly, the healthier your body is, the easier it is for you to manifest what you want in this reality. When your body reaches a healthy state, you are more receptive to knowledge, energy, wisdom, and blessings. Toxicity in your foods can cause blockages and imbalances within your temple. If you take care of your body, your body will take care of you, babe.

Recite your mantras and remember to feel grateful and thankful as if your dream is already your reality.

Yoni Mantras

I am stepping confidently into my greatness. Abundance flows to me.

I am vibrating on the frequency of all that I desire.

All necessary tools, resources, and knowledge are at my disposal. I can manifest all things I desire.

I can manifest all things through my divine power. I ask you for what I desire, and the universe provides.

I am receiving all I desire.

Manifesting is my divine right. I am attracting
wealth, health, and abundance.

I give myself permission to be successful.
I am resonating at a high frequency.

My greatest blessings are on their way to me.

I have the power to create my own destiny. I am
capable of receiving whatever my heart desires.

My womb is a clear energy field, and it is
easy for me to receive inner guidance.

My goals will manifest within and outside of me.

I am attracting like-minded individuals.
I am vibrating at a higher frequency.

It is easy to manifest my desires through my
thoughts, prayers, actions, and meditations.

I am connected to my power to create. My womb and mind
are safe spaces for all of my creativity and authenticity.

I deserve to have a beautiful home, a loving family,
financial freedom, and unlimited manifestations.

My womb is free of all blockages. I am
free to powerfully manifest all things.

I am attracting peace, prosperity, health, and happiness.

The magic inside of me is powerful.

I am confident in my growing abilities. I am
open and willing to learn and grow.

I believe in miracles. Miracles are taking place all around me.

I can have anything my heart desires. Movement
and change are helping me grow.

Sacred Healing Practice

This healing practice will require you to sacrifice a little bit of sleep. It is best to meditate between the hours of 4 a.m. and 7 a.m. Meditation benefits are enhanced when your mind is free, your stomach is empty, and your body is rejuvenated. If meditating that early in the morning is not feasible for you, feel free to meditate when you first wake up or right before you go to sleep at night.

The act of meditating causes our pituitary gland to release endorphins. Endorphins raise our vibration and allow us to feel good, physically and emotionally. After meditating, you will find you have set a calm tone and will have more energy to take on the day. This meditation can be performed with your hands placed over your womb while laying down on your back or sitting up with aligned posture and your palms facing the sky. When our palms are facing the sky, we are more open to receiving our blessings in abundance. A bonus to this exercise is to try to meditate outdoors. Spending time in nature is amazing for your overall well-being.

Select your desired position and get comfortable. Ensure the temperature of the room is just right, your clothes are comfortable, and you are focused on your manifestation meditation. You are free to meditate in silence or with soft music in the background. There are many amazing guided meditations on YouTube that will show you how to relax your mind, scan your body, and reach a deep meditative state. You can also enhance your meditation experience by lighting a candle, journaling prior to your session, or surrounding yourself with healing crystals.

In your meditation, start off by expressing appreciation for your current blessings. Focus on your breath. Continue by using your imagination to visualize what it is you desire. Hold the image in your mind as you get excited about your manifestation! See yourself smiling, laughing, and in love with life.

Read the affirmations below and feel your energy connecting to the earth.

I am so blessed.
I am attracting wealth, health, love, and abundance.
All of my deepest desires are coming to fruition.
I am ready to receive, and I am ready to give.
My account balances are increasing.
I am generating multiple streams of income.
My body is perfectly balanced.
I am fully at peace.
Love is attracted to me, and I am attracted to love.
I am ready to manifest all I desire.
Thank you, thank you, thank you.

Tap into Your Goddess
Body with Me

www.yonimuse.com

Embody Empress Energy

Join me on a consistent basis as we tap into our goddess body and heal from within. Each masterclass has a specific intention for the week. We will be welcoming abundance, peace, love, prosperity, and expansion on all levels.

I also teach dance and sensual movement during sessions. I also offer weekly sound baths for clients. Be sure to tap in with your headphones to receive and feel the healing vibrations virtually. I'll see you in class!

Yoni Muse Collection

The Yoni Muse Collection is designed specifically for feminine and sacred body parts. The collection includes a healing yoni bawm, yoni complexion scrub, yoni steams, body oil, herbal salt cleanses, and waist beads. My external based products are designed to keep your yoni pretty and well-groomed. This is the perfect collection to use before an intimate night or as a sexy addition to your self-care routine. This product collection is highly demanded by my goddesses, so be sure to join our email list for restock alerts at www.yonimuse.com.

Healing and Meditative Retreats

Vibe with me in person! Let's connect on a deeper level. My healing retreats are full of relaxation, peace, and sensuality. Give your heart, mind, body, and spirit the time and attention they need. You will be poured a glass of wine or a refreshing green juice before your healing massage. You will unleash your inner goddess through sensual dancing and yoga. Come free yourself and nurture your temple.

Intuitive Readings

Using my psychic gifts and intuitive abilities, I offer personal readings to empresses seeking guidance on their path. Always be sure to consult your own intuition about life choices first. All the answers you need are already within you. Readings are designed to channel your energy and provide insight on your current vibration. Your reading is simply confirmation of what you already know, or will remember.

My personal readings are delivered through text, so you can keep them for your own wisdom and guidance. You are welcome to connect with me through video as well, whichever you are most comfortable with. My goal is to use my gift to heal and teach manifestation to my soul tribe. This sacred gift I have has changed my life, and I want to share it with you.

Peace and Love,
Jewel the Muse

Conclusion

To conclude, I want to express my appreciation for your support and trust along this journey. Keep *Yoni Mantras* close to your heart and share it with your goddess sisters. This book will always be a reminder of your womb magic, femininity, and sacredness.

I wish you well, and I pray you and I will be able to connect on a deeper level for years to come. I will continue to allow the divine to work through me to provide you with all my tools, guidance, and pure love.

Flip to the book index for information regarding my product line. Be blessed, Goddess, and welcome to a whole new world.

Ase and Alhamdulillah!

@theyonimuse
www.yonimuse.com

Thank you for reading
*Yoni Mantras: An empress's guide to peace within
the heart, temple, and sacred womb.*
If you enjoyed this book, please leave an online review.

About the Author

Jewel the Muse is a dancer, yogi, and holistic advocate for women across the globe. She is an author, entrepreneur, and spiritual goddess. Her life's purpose is to help women channel find peace within their heart, temple, and sacred wombs.

Her brand, Yoni Muse, was crafted to be a safe haven for women to connect and heal their full body. Yoni Muse includes a feminine wellness product line, books, retreats, and coaching sessions.

CPSIA information can be obtained
at www.ICGtesting.com
Printed in the USA
BVHW051256230323
661008BV00016B/612